ANDORRA REVEALED

An Anthology

Paperback First-Edition.

First published in 2016

ISBN 978-999203079-0

ABOUT THE BOOK

Welcome to *Andorra Revealed*. Come with us and we will take you on a journey, through fact and fiction, memoire and imagination, behind the scenes and into the heart of this unique, pocket-sized country. This is not a guide book as such – you can find information about the country's 625 restaurants and 330 hotels with a couple of clicks on the Internet. No, this is both an entertaining companion for would-be visitors and a practical guide for those considering Andorra as a place to live.

The book is crammed with facts about the country, past and present, interwoven with bedtime stories that reveal even more of this rare Co-Princedom: tales of smugglers and pigs, murder and even witches on broomsticks, punctuated here and there by elegant haikus and cheeky limericks. This is a travel book like no other, eccentric and eclectic, sharing with you the allure that has brought foreigners from all over the world to make this country their home.

None more so than the authors themselves: Clare Allcard arrived by sailboat - and finally car - from Singapore, Judith Wood, born in Bombay, was drawn from London, Iain Woolward from Silicon Valley, Alexandra Grebennikova from Russia, Valerie Rymarenko from Catalonia while Ursula Simpson Ure was born in Shanghai, brought up in Cairo and arrived in Andorra by camper van from London. Between them they have lived in Andorra a total of 133 years.

SPRING

SUMMER

AUTUMN (and back to Winter)

AN INTRODUCTION

Several hundred times
I've walked that mountain track, and
still it pleases me.

Valerie Rymarenko

ANDORRA AT A GLANCE:

Country name: Principality of Andorra, or simply Andorra

Andorran country name: Principat d'Andorra

Country's borders: A 120.3 km circle of 65 mountain peaks rising above 2,500m. France stretches for 56.6kms to the north, Spain 63.7km to the south. Only here, at the border crossing, does the frontier dip below 1,000m.

Size: 468 km square

Highest mountain: Comapedrosa, 2,942m

Lowest point: 840m

Population: 76,098 (2013) of whom 34,989 were Andorran; 20,070 Spanish; 10,809 Portuguese; 3,695 French; 970 British; 628 Argentinean; 312 German; 97 North American.

***Comuns* or Parishes - in order of precedence:** Canillo, Encamp, Ordino, La Massana, Andorra la Vella, Sant Julià de Lòria, Escaldes-Engordany. (Andorran parishes or *comuns* are not just ecclesiastical enclaves but are administrative divisions having a local election for mayor and council every four years.)

Capital: Andorra la Vella (at 1,023m, the highest capital in Europe).

Other towns: Canillo, Encamp, Ordino, La Massana, Sant Julià, Escaldes, Pas de la Casa and Santa Coloma.

Official language: Catalan with Spanish and French widely spoken and English growing in recognition by the day.

Religion: Some 90% are nominal Catholics

Currency: Euro

Head of Government: (at the time of writing) Antoni Martí

Head of State: (at the time of writing) **Co-Princes** The President of France, (François Hollande) and His Serene Highness, the Archbishop of Urgell, Joan Enric Vives Sicilia.

Defence: In case of need all Andorran men with firearms theoretically can be called to serve, but without remuneration.

National parks and nature reserves: The first two protected areas were Xixerella and Enclar. In 2004 the Valley of Madriu-Perafita-Claror (4,247 hectares, a little over 9% of the national territory) was declared a UNESCO World Heritage site. There are also national parks at Comapedrosa and Sorteny.

Protected species: include the chamois, the wolf and brown bear.

Flora & fauna: Some 1,643 species of flowers/grasses and 60 of fauna.

Butterflies: Around 156 species at the last count.

Birds: The official Andorran list notes 172 species including the Capercaille, Lammergeier, Snowfinch, Wallcreeper and the rarely seen Tengmalm's Owl.

International telephone code: +376

Time: CET (GMT + 1 hour)

Tourist board web site:
http://visitandorra.com/en/home/ plus the app Andorra Go!

Public Holidays: 1st January (New Year's Day); 6th January (Three Kings/ Epiphany); 14th March (Constitution Day); Easter Day; 1st May (Labour Day); Ascension Day; Whit Monday, 24th June (St John's Eve); 15th August (Assumption); 8th September (Meritxell National Day); 1st November (All Saints Day); 8th December (Immaculate Conception); 24th & 25th December (Christmas Eve and Christmas Day); 31st December (New Year's Eve). During the summer most Andorran villages have their own colourful street *festa*.

Shopping: Most shops only close on 14th March; 8th September; Christmas Day and New Year's Day.

Opening hours: Anything between 9am and 9pm with the smaller shops closing for lunch between 1pm – 4pm (or 5pm).

THE LAND OF FREE FESTIVALS!

Locals and visitors alike delight in Andorra's abundance of festivals – almost all of which are free. During the summer even the tiniest hamlet has its *Festa Major* which can last anywhere from two to five days and run on well into the wee hours of the morning. I put this down to the fact that the seven parishes of Andorra have as intense a 'festival' rivalry as the 'rugby' rivalry of the four nations of the United Kingdom, striving to outdo each other with the number of events they can pack into 24 hours. Mobile discos often *start* at 4am!

As well as the village fêtes, nearly all of which are packed into the summer months, Andorra enjoys major feast days throughout the year with the parishes again competing to put on the best show in town.

A FESTIVE CALENDAR

1) 31st December/1st January. People gather in bars and homes all over Andorra and Spain to see the New Year in. 12 grapes are eaten in time to the twelve strikes of the clock marking the last moments of the old year while toasts drunk in cava or champagne welcome in the new.

2) 5th/6th January. Twelfth Night/ Epiphany/ Three Kings/ Reis Traditional time for giving children presents. Accompanied by street pageants, floats and special three Kings cakes.

3) 17th January: The Feast of Sant Antoni and the Pig or the Day of the Free Lunch. Open air feast of rich meat stew served up from huge cauldrons heated by wood fires and washed down with red wine.

4) Carnival Celebrations start about a week before Lent with parades, fancy dress competitions and balls and the hanging of Carnestoltes – the figure of Carnival.

5) 23rd April: Sant Jordi (Saint George's): the Day of the Book and the Rose. The day when traditionally all females give the males they love books and all males give the love of their heart a red rose.

6) Palm Sunday & Easter Intricately woven palms for girls and plain palms for boys, given to them by their godmothers, are blessed and carried into church on Palm Sunday. Apart from Mass, Easter Day is celebrated with special, highly decorated cakes called Mona given to the children by their godfathers. Groups go from house to house singing Caramelles and collecting donations of eggs or money.

7) 23rd June: Eve of Sant Joan. Andorra's equivalent of the British Bonfire Night. Fires are lit all over Andorra and Catalonia for this celebration of Summer's Solstice. And, of course, there's a special cake too.

8) 8th September: Meritxell Day. The country's national saint's day in honour of the country's patron saint, Our Lady of Meritxell. All shops are closed and thousands go to the Sanctuary of Meritxell to celebrate.

9) 31st October/1st November: Castanyada/All Saints. The time to feast on roasted chestnuts bought off carts in the streets and delicious little marzipan confections called *panellets*. It is also when people go to the family graves to clean them up and decorate them with potted chrysanthemums.

10) 24th December: Christmas Eve Father Christmas visits all the parishes. Missa del Gall /Midnight Mass and "Caga Tió" (*"Shit log"*!)

ANDORRA: AN HISTORICAL PERSPECTIVE.

A work of quasi-fiction by Iain Woolward

The phone rang. "Hola, eees dat Senior Ponsonby?" "Ponsonby-*Smythe*" I answered. I was about to be invited to Andorra - a country of which I had barely heard - to perform in what I was told was a celebration concert of some saint's day or other. The caller already knew that the Philharmonic, in which I played second violin, would be on its summer break and quickly offered a persuasive fee (plus expenses) with a directness that suggested he already knew I was in no position to refuse. Within the hour I had booked my travel and was Googling and Wiki'ing 'Andorra' so as not to appear a total ignoramus upon my arrival.

A month later I landed at Barcelona airport and transferred to what seemed like an inordinately small bus for an inordinately long journey north, up into the Pyrenees, to Andorra. Naturally I grabbed one of the few unoccupied double seats, dumping myself in one and my baggage and violin case on the other so as to discourage any last minute passengers from reducing the already skimpy elbow room I was to occupy for the next two or three hours. All I needed after the enforced scrummage of a deep-discount flight from Gatwick (few classical musicians fly full-fare, and even fewer second violinists), was to deal with the persistent nudging and withering breath of some smelly old peasant bearing a crate of chickens or whatever else one might expect of remote mountain people.

Alas, to no avail. Seconds prior to departure a wizened old man, panting heavily but thankfully devoid of chickens, politely awaited the removal of my belongings and flopped down beside me, in the last remaining seat.

The first hour or so of our journey was passed in silence. Then the intensity with which I was staring at the mountainous terrain that our little bus was expected to ascend prompted my neighbour to enquire in an accented English that he somehow already knew was my native tongue, 'Sir, this is the first time you have travelled to Andorra, yes?' Turning to him somewhat regretfully ... what could I possibly have in common with this person? ... I nodded in the affirmative. Unfortunately, this was sufficient to invoke a monologue. "You will enjoy Andorra, I think. Your country ... England, perhaps? ... and mine, have much in common. Yours: an island in the sea. Mine: in the mountains. Both very independent ... mine a little older as a nation..." His gaze wandered off slightly as if he was reminiscing from his personal past. The slightest of smiles hinted that he was politely but decidedly edging me into an exchange of views.

I obliged. "I'm sure Andorra is a very wonderful little country and all that, but you do realize that the history of England as a nation dates back over a thousand years ...?"

"Ah yes ... Athelstan." He then provided a silence in which the immediacy and accuracy of his answer could go to work on my tired mind. Given the sense of superiority with which my breeding and education had been designed to endow me, I was unaccustomed to such attempts at intellectual rivalry. I sat up in my seat and proceeded with more caution.

"Yes, indeed. 939 A.D. The first king of all England and all that, hmmmm …" My voice wavered then faded weakly without addressing, let alone dismissing, the 'oldest nation' jibe. Lacking the knowledge with which to rebut, I hesitated. The opposition did not.

"Your Athelstan, he was a good man, but this was nearly 150 years after Charlemagne confirmed sovereignty upon Andorra … by then a country whose borders had stood firm since, well … since national borders formalized the tribal territories that formed not long after the retreat of the Ice Age …" More gaze-wandering, slight smiling and so on.

My mind flicked to 'The Hustler' - the film in which Paul Newman's character sucks winnings out of losers by feigning to be one. I shifted uneasily in my seat and settled on a position whereby I could look down my nose at my adversary. This gave me a moment to try to figure out how to grope or bluff my way off the ropes. "Yes, indeed. Good old Charlemagne. First class chap. But there is, of course, the slight matter of 'democracy'. I *think* I'm correct in saying that, at 1215, our Magna Carta is the world's first democratic declaration?" said I, entirely rhetorically.

"Quite so, quite so. But then, if a country – like Andorra for example – avoids being ruled by tyrants altogether, then it does not need a document with which to control their powers, no?"

This was becoming the Rachmaninoff of casual conversations. I'd have to sharpen my wits considerably, or acknowledge defeat from under a stiff upper lip. "Yes," I acknowledged, "but all constitutional democracies start short of their ultimate form … even in America." By now I was almost flinching in anticipation of the next volley.

"But, Sir, how can you compare your country to America in this regard? American democracy is protected by a legal document ...The Constitution; your country has none."

"And Andorra ...?" asked I, remembering vaguely that this might be a point of weakness.

"It is true. While our country is one of the world's oldest, its constitution is one of the youngest ... 1993. Maybe England, too, will have such a thing one day ...?"

"Well, as Dame Margaret Thatcher once said, 'Who needs a constitution when one is already endowed with common sense?'"

"Yes, she would say a thing like that," was the withering response. Again, silence.

The bus had been whipping along up to this point, but now slowed to walking speed at the customs post between Spain and Andorra, through which traffic was progressing slowly but surely. The same could not be said for the opposite direction. The traffic bound for Spain was backed up a kilometre or so. This gave me an opportunity for a diversionary tactic - and possibly a counter attack. "Is the Spanish border often so slow?"

"Sometimes it is so. Andorra has the lowest sales taxes in all of Europe; our neighbours are constantly struggling to stop smuggling by their own people, burdened as they are by sales taxes as much as six times higher than those of Andorra".

"It is a wonder that neither Spain nor France has ever simply occupied Andorra and be done with it!" Yes! Parry that you annoying little man!

"Well, my little country was obliged to take a different road to freedom than yours. Not a shot has been fired, nor a tax levied to pay for the defence of our independence. In stormy times, we merely bent to the breeze and waited for a change in the weather."

Generally unimpressed with analogies, I was encouraged in my attack; armed by my Googling, I attempted to corner my opponent in an inconsistency: "Yes, indeed. Perhaps this is why, on the one hand you brag about having side-stepped tyrannical monarchs, but today we find not just one, but two 'Princes' atop your 'Co-Principality': the French President and a Spanish Bishop! Foreigners, no less!"

"Exactly." Silence.

"But, if England had gone down *that* road, Buckingham Palace would be shared by the descendants of Julius Caesar and Eric Bloodaxe!"

"And which would it have been?"

"… but that's beside the point!"

"No, sir. It *is* the point. In Andorra's experience, opposing Princes of equal weight neutralize each other."

"That's all very well to say …" I sputtered, trying to summon up a rebuttal to a point so economically phrased I was pushed to parse it. Too late...

"We Andorrans read about your Great King Harold and we shake our heads. In a matter of – how do you English say – a 'fortnight' he lost your country's fleeting independence by doing exactly the opposite of what we Andorrans were doing at that time: he destroyed the very balance of power that we were nourishing: he crushed a Viking incursion …"

"And rid England of those barbaric tyrants!!"

"Precisely. Like Andorra, you had two great empires contesting your territory. The Vikings had already extended trade routes clear across modern-day Europe to the Black Sea; the Normans controlled most of coastal Europe. But at that time the English were barely a nation, let alone an empire. So what does Harold do? He breaks off preparations to defend his realm from the oncoming Normans, rushes north to beat back a few thousand Vikings … maybe because his brother joined them after losing the competition for the English throne, yes? Upon hitting the beach in England, William could not believe his luck! Not only was he relieved of the very considerable task of fighting the mighty Vikings for control of England; the much less formidable English were now so exhausted they were destroyed in just over an hour at Hastings. Where England had Vikings and Normans, Andorra had ... and still has ... the Spanish and the French. Our strategy, even to this day, has been to maintain a balance of power in which, to win control of our little country, one great power would have to take on another. This France and Spain have declined to do."

Again, silence was provided in which I could have rallied, but failing to do so, the onslaught continued ...

"… And, if I may add sir, there is no more expensive way to resolve conflict than battling it out militarily. Throughout your country's history your countrymen have been frequently and repeatedly taxed to breaking point just to pay for wars, the fighting of which was somehow considered glorious. And once governments start sucking, as they say, 'on the tit of taxes' they become addicted!"

I was much relieved as, at that moment, the bus pulled into its terminus in Andorra La Vella – a town that appeared to be cleaner, more orderly, and at least as prosperous as any in Western Europe. I muttered what I hoped would be a conclusive, "Ah. Here we are." But, being intrigued by the worthiness of my opponent, I couldn't help but turn to him as we shuffled off the bus and ask, "By the way, what was it you do again?"

"I'm a piano player; I'm returning briefly to my homeland to perform Rachmaninoff's third concerto in d minor tomorrow evening at the Centre de Congressos, here in Andorra la Vella. Perhaps you'd like to come along?"

FISCAL FUNDAMENTALS AND TOURIST BLING

by Iain Woolward

"Can you write an entertaining piece about the financial side of life in Andorra?" they asked. "Oh, no problem," I deadpanned. "After all, look at all the great literature that has sprung from the tax codes of the western world."

If you've read this far you're probably aware that all financial articles begin or end with riveting stuff like: 'In no way should advice and recommendations in this article be construed as such. Opinions expressed herein are the random musings of the author and may bring about personal bankruptcy. Never take responsibility for your own financial affairs without seeking prior guidance from a professional to whom you've paid sufficient inducement for him/her to be held at least semi-accountable. And, whatever you do, don't come bitching to the author if this article turns out to be a bunch of misguided twaddle: he/she is simply pushing a particular viewpoint exclusively for personal gain.'

This article isn't like that.

I'll tell you what I've learned, fiscally speaking, from becoming a Passive (non-working) Resident in Andorra. My only caveat is that the situation is changing rapidly as I write (late-2015).

Keeping What You've Got

Notwithstanding the country's many fine attributes, most Passive Residents in Andorra came here with the preservation of capital firmly in mind. While their chances of doing so have slightly diminished recently with the introduction of a 10% income tax, Andorra still provides an extremely friendly tax environment. For example, neither capital gains nor inheritances are taxed. Also, there is no 'wealth tax' (i.e. a tax on the total assets you've worked hard to accumulate over the years). Sales taxes are about a sixth of those of Andorra's European neighbours.

The primary reason Andorra even introduced an income tax was not to reduce a withering deficit of the type now commonplace in western democracies. Andorra is better managed than that. It was to secure double-taxation treaties from its tax-addicted neighbours. By the time you read this, Andorra should have concluded agreements with a respectably lengthy list of countries whereby, roughly speaking, taxes paid in those countries can be deducted from tax owed in Andorra, and vice versa.

I'd tell you about the laboriousness (or otherwise) of the tax-paying process in Andorra, but that's still being worked out as I write.

Getting In

To benefit from that benign tax situation one has to be a Fiscal (or tax-paying) Resident of Andorra, a prerequisite for which is to be accepted as a Passive Resident. To qualify as such you'll have to prove you are a law-abiding citizen who can pay your own way come what may, in sickness and in health. Oh….and you'll need to make an investment of 400,000 Euros in an Andorra residence, business or investment vehicle. About 10% of that money is earmarked as an interest-free bond, forfeitable should you misbehave while residing here, but returnable should you leave without misbehaving. Meanwhile you are required to spend at least 90 days a year here. Note: Andorran customs officers generally look deceptively casual; that's partly because CCTV cameras copiously record all movement in and out of the country.

Banking

Historically, most Passive Residents have kept their relationships with local banks to local bill-paying. (Regular bills are generally debited directly without an invoice being issued). They do this because the banks here have a history of extracting eye-watering fees; and, as attested by swanky offices and branches, they're masters at it. But if, having reviewed credit rating agency data (Andorran banks rank amongst the best capitalized in the world), you decide to take Andorran banks more seriously, the next step is to have an eyeball-to-eyeball meeting with your prospective banker regarding fees. In Andorra you can…and are expected to….negotiate case-by-case terms. In my experience, a bloody-minded client can pester his way to reasonably competitive charges, by 'private banking' standards. A simple rule of thumb is: don't put money into an Andorran bank unless and until you have confirmed in writing exactly what it will cost to deploy it elsewhere.

The implication of privacy in 'Private' banking is pretty redundant these days; Andorra signed up to international anti-money laundering disclosure rules years ago. But they do deliver exceptionally well on the level of personal service implicit in the term 'private'. They are also well equipped to serve customers online. The one big 'online' exception is the trading of equities: that is still – at time of writing - an offline service and priced accordingly.

The one big *potential* caveat to all of the above is that, in April 2015, one Andorran bank (the now defunct Banca Privada Andorra – 'BPA') was attacked by the U.S. government for money laundering in which the bank had indulged three years earlier. Notwithstanding the fact that steps had already been taken in Andorra to correct the problem with best-in-class anti-money laundering practices, the U.S. issued a highly negative and thoroughly out-dated press release that, in a 'stroke of the pen', stripped BPA of its correspondent banking relationships in the U.S. This put the highly solvent bank out of business. (If BPA had been, say, UBS or Barclays, a simple fine would have been levied after wrong doing had been acknowledged or proven in court. No such luck for BPA.) In order to uphold the viability of the remaining Andorran banks and to curry favour with the U.S. Feds., the Andorran government paid millions to a global accounting firm to re-audit the source of funds of every BPA client (about 25,000, of whom approximately 24,997 were proved to be perfectly law-abiding citizens). While this auditing was going on and a 'Good Bank' could be formed out of the ashes of the 'Bad Bank' all client accounts were frozen, other than a small weekly cash withdrawal allowance to pay bills. As I write (eight months after the U.S. attack) BPA customers have yet to regain control of 'their' property. If the value of those assets has dropped in the meanwhile, tough luck. Regardless of the merits of the injustices involved, the Andorran government has neither the stomach nor the resources to take on the U.S. Feds on behalf of those who entrusted their assets to one of the country's banks.

The good news is, of course, that the very fact that such a thing happened almost ensures that it won't reoccur. The colourful shenanigans of some of Andorra's banks are now but distant echoes in the corridors of their still-plush headquarters. Global finance has changed, and Andorran banking right along with it.

Housing

There's good news and bad news when it comes to the Andorran property market. Both are summed up in the term 'zero cost of ownership'. Other than the cost of buying a home, in Andorra it costs virtually nothing to own it. Goodness, right? Not necessarily. The problem is that the property market is loaded with highly-imaginatively priced homes – ninety per cent of which are apartments - that linger on the market for years in the hope that some cash-laden new arrivals will actually pay the asking price. Actual sale prices are not published, so both buyers and sellers are fumbling around in the dark as regards comparables. Most new Passive Residents tend to rent for their first few years while they figure things out. There's a huge inventory of rentable apartments – but the stock of detached houses for rent is very limited indeed.

A word of warning on Andorran apartments: test the sound insulation before committing. A lot of them don't have any. When Andorra experienced a building boom a few decades ago, apartment buildings shot up like weeds. Building regulations required that natural stone finishes be applied to much of their exteriors, but behind these facades often lies a very rudimentary reinforced concrete structure with no between-floors insulation.

Wheels

Andorra is picky about cars, which is why you don't see abandoned ones littered around the place. Only relatively new cars may be imported (currently paying around 4.5% duty en route). However, Andorran dealers provide a wide selection of fairly-priced, 'pre-owned' vehicles. (Good thing about living in a tiny country: word of dodgy practice gets around at lightning speed and there's nowhere to hide if you've ripped someone off). Unless you have a good reason for doing otherwise, buy a 4-wheel drive car. Recently penalties were introduced in Andorra for driving in snow with a car deemed unfit for purpose (i.e. 2-wheel drive; no chains). The road system in Andorra is excellent, but not much of it is flat, especially in the north of the country. Even if your 2-wheel drive car can get up snowy inclines, getting down them can go horribly wrong in a thudding heartbeat. The seasoned locals get a tad irritated at being held up by white knuckled recent-arrivals inching along at walking speed, caught out by the foot of snow that fell out of the sky while they were having dinner somewhere. And even though the roads are ploughed with commendable – possibly incomparable - efficiency, the unprepared quickly become the unwelcome.

Bling

Annually there are about 10 million 'visits' to Andorra. Many are for skiing, hiking or just gazing up at the high places where one could be doing those things were one not sitting on a pleasant terrace enjoying a sangria strong enough to weaken the knees. But a large percentage of visitors come just to shop, relatively tax-free - there is no value-added tax in Andorra. During Europe's extensive holiday season, busloads of tourists, urgency in their eyes, disgorge daily into the two main shopping precincts: Andorra La Vella/Escaldes-Engordany in the centre of the country for a 'high street' experience and a super-store area close to the Spanish border. Compared to the rest of Europe, alcohol and tobacco are so cheap that the enforcement of duty-free limits is practiced in industrial proportions by customs inspectors in neighbouring France and Spain. Global-brand 'luxury' items - RayBan sunglasses, Chanel No° 5 perfume, Longchamp wallets – all the goodies you'd find in the duty free area of a leading international airport plus a vast array of electronics – get snatched off Andorran shelves in bulk. The bonanza includes wonderfully ethnic food products; don't be surprised to see haunches of exotically smoked pig displayed cheek by jowl with Versace, Bvlgari, Cartier and Mikimoto. Yum, yum.

Pedestrian-friendly shopping areas are interspersed with inviting, spotless cafes. Shopping hours are generous: typically 9.00 or 9.30am until 9.00pm. (But check opening hours for Spanish-style lunchtime closing). Many shops are open on Sundays until 8.00pm.

But even the un-taxed needs to be un-stocked periodically. Sales occur twice a year and November is the prime promotional month, nationwide. That's when those who live here can pounce on special discounts. My wife's closet boasts names like Valentino and Armani that, I can assure you, would never have made it there without 75% discounts off tax-free prices. I'm told the fun about shopping in Andorra is as much about conquest as ownership....the sheer joy of seeing items that you know cost orders of magnitude more on the renowned shopping boulevards of Europe. The equivalent streets in Andorra ring with the delighted jabbering of acquisitive females, giggling like schoolgirls as they haul their kill off to some tavern or café to plot an event at which they can display their winnings. And there is no shortage of such opportunities in Andorra: dinner/dances, live concerts, visiting ballet companies; Andorra is dynamic. Women can even wear hats relatively inconspicuously....which wasn't necessarily what they had in mind when they bought them. It's unclear if the gaiety is a throwback to more formal days or a confident statement about the future. Either way it's goodness.

The Basics: Food, etc.

Most of the time, of course, shopping consists of trudging up and down grocery aisles. Other than a local coffee brand and whatever Andorran tobacco (the primary crop hereabouts) finds its way back to its homeland by way of cigarette factories elsewhere, little you can buy in Andorra originates in here. 'Fresh' vegetables have been trucked in and are priced accordingly. Fish gets hauled up from sea level for purchase on Tuesdays and Fridays. Choice can be limited. Fresh sweet corn, for example, is hard to come by. On a given day the nearest spring onion might be a round-trip away, immediately across the border in La Seu, Spain. And so one adjusts what one cooks and how one cooks it. Please take note: those footnotes in recipe books about cooking at altitude are true; boiling an egg takes considerably longer in Andorra than at sea level because the water boils at a deceptively and significantly lower temperature. Ovens, too, seem to operate at a more leisurely pace than that of their cousins at lower altitudes. Darned if I know why.

Moving to Andorra requires a certain sense of adventure and most new arrivals are an international lot, well-practiced in culinary improvisation. In any case, the stalls in the Tuesday and Saturday markets in La Seu – just across the Spanish border - bow under the weight of fresh fruit and vegetables, fine olive oils and vinegars; hundreds of cheeses; multiple flavours of honey and sweet preserves; myriads of different breads.....and so on. Then there are the cured meats from every part of locally-reared livestock - and I do mean 'every': some are a better source of smutty humour than nutritional value.

Should you feel like getting out of the mountains for a while, a trip to Barcelona's markets - la Boqueria, Mercat de Sant Antoni and Santa Caterina - provide even more choice: hundreds of stalls of sparkling fresh sea food and creatively inspired tapas to see you through the drive back to your Andorran kitchen with a boot-load of goodies. Salut!

Three ladies saw a ballet in La Vella
And liked the prima ballerina
But later over tea
It was interesting to see
*They'd **adored** the young men's posteria.*

A Bow to King Boris

by Alexandra Grebennikova

Have you ever heard of Boris Skossyreff? He was a Russian émigré escaped from the Revolution who allegedly proclaimed himself Boris I, the King of Andorra, and ruled the country for eleven days.

Andorra is a country of silences. The buzz of traffic and the presence of boisterous tourists doesn't manage to upset them: the silences just grow stronger. All of my favourite Andorrans – by which I mean, those who were born in Andorra, both children of immigrants and indigenous people – have the weirdest local gift of never letting you bring up whatever it is they prefer to ignore. They have the power of keeping quiet the way the rocks keep quiet, the way the river that hones the rocks doesn't share its views and the monotonous noise of the wind never answers a question. They are the children of the mountain: they'll only tell you what they really want to say. Their concept of freedom of speech is, first and foremost, the freedom of unrestricted silence, the choice to be discreet. The Catalan expression that could be translated as "doing as Andorrans do" means "make believe you didn't understand the question", "convince the others that you are as simple as a child", "pretend you don't have anything to do with the world and its troubles". It doesn't mean they are in any way naïve. Under particular circumstances, they can be as ruthless as the Germans and as cunning as the Swiss; they are often courageous and faithful; they may like or dislike talking as a pastime. Nonetheless, it is they who will decide what they want to talk about, and a part of their souls always stays undiscovered, veiled from a foreigner, no matter how long you stay with them or how much they like you. They cannot help it, much in the same way as I can't help showing and saying what I think, what I defend and what I am. That is probably why they never really accept a foreigner as one of their equals: in order to become a true Andorran, you need to be Andorran in the third generation. They are accustomed to foreign eccentricities. I came to love them, and we peacefully coexist. They let me talk, they sometimes tell me stories, and I never get too frustrated if my questions stay unanswered. After a decade or so I've become accustomed to their world, and still feel comfortable inside the mountain, between the mountains, surrounded by mountains and in all kinds of mountain settings.

Every time I've tried to understand the story of Boris I, the King of Andorra, I've been confronted with the kind of silence you face when you try to discuss corruption, witchery, obscure and unresolved crimes or buried disputes. I've read different versions of Boris Skossyreff's Andorran adventure and I still don't know who exactly he was, what he was, how he came to gain such extraordinary and short-lived influence in the Valleys. Other questions I'd like to be able to answer (but can't) are, for example, who benefited from his presence in the country and why did nobody try to defend or hide him when the Spanish gendarmes arrested the "King" on Andorran territory in the name of Spanish law. How did he manage to get Andorran citizenship in December 1933, and did he really manage to get it? Maybe nobody really knows what happened in the months of May, June and July 1934. In truth, what kind of a madman do you have to be to propose yourself as a possible monarch to the people of a foreign country? I have to mention, though, that Boris's design was not entirely original. According to the press, there were two or three other people who tried to become "King of Andorra" in exchange for a substantial sum of money, but were rejected. It obviously helped that Boris was an elegant Russian of aristocratic descent, but even so, it's hard to believe he set off on such a dangerous adventure entirely on his own. He must have had some foreign and national support, and I can't help thinking he served as a puppet in some kind of a game of complex interests that I still haven't come to understand.

Boris Skossyreff was born in Vilnius, formerly a part of the Russian empire and currently the capital of independent Lithuania (though some of the papers described him as "a young Pole"). With his expensive suits and golf pants, he produced the impression of a perfect foreign gentleman, very British. He was a ladies' man. During his stay in Andorra, two of his lovers were there with him, one of them English, the other one American. His English lover, Polly, or Phyllis, stayed in the picturesque village of Santa Coloma. The American, Florence Marmon, was the one who accompanied him to the mass offered by Bishop

Guitart at the cathedral of La Seu d'Urgell to commemorate the death of the Catalan president Francesc Macià. The Andorran historian David Mas considers that Boris might have created the persona of a "Count of Orange" with the sole purpose of seducing and conquering Florence Marmon.

The international journalists adored Boris Skossyreff. When he was already in a Spanish prison, the New York Times correspondent wrote the much-quoted lines: "Although wearing the blue overalls issued to all Spanish prisoners, and with his ever-present monocle in his right eye, Boris de Skossyreff, … pretender to the throne of Andorra, preserved much of his royal dignity and air of distinction…" Where this royal dignity and distinction originally came from, is hard to tell. One thing we know for sure: Boris Skossyreff was a brilliant liar. We don't know whether he was a compulsive liar or a well-trained liar, an amateur or a professional, but he was definitely a liar of a kind. Even his date of birth varies depending on the sources. We don't really know where he was arrested after declaring war on a co-prince of Andorra. One of the versions of the story actually claims it happened in La Seu d'Urgell where the bishop had invited him to the solemn mass at the cathedral, on July 20, 1934. If that is true, it means that he decided to accept the Bishop's invitation after declaring war on him, which was unwise but totally in the spirit of a romantic adventure, which marked his entire Andorran crusade.

There is good evidence that in his later life Boris joined the Nazi party in Germany, though he couldn't have been German, and only Germans were accepted in it, fought against Russians in the Second World War and was arrested by the Soviets in 1948. It seems that he spent about eight years in the Soviet Gulag, to be returned to Germany after the death of Stalin. When he arrived in Germany, he divorced his first wife, Marie-Louise Parat and married a German forty years younger than him, by the name of Maria Roswitha. He had a fascinating life full of inexplicable contradictions. The only thing we seem to know for sure is the date of his death in Boppard, Germany, 55 years after the Andorran adventure. Much to my disappointment, he doesn't seem to have talked much about Andorra after the 1930s. He probably tried to forget everything about it once it stopped being his kingdom. Andorra is a magical, wonderful corner of the Pyrenees, as anyone who has ever lived here knows, but its very smallness makes it prone to be left behind and forgotten. Most people who have loved it and chosen to forget it will confirm how easy it is to hide its image behind the other places that populate their memory.

Boris Skossyreff could have been an international spy though it's the one thing he probably wasn't. His brilliant command of foreign languages and the extraordinary capacity he had to get away from all kinds of police investigations of his person speak in favour of it. However, he was too poor, too desperate for money to qualify as a James Bond of the period. Professional spies do not forge cheques or steal gold watches, or do they sometimes? What do we really know about the international spies' profiles? "They spy on people for money all the time", so they shouldn't be trusted, as one of the main characters of a popular television series recently put it. In any case, they shouldn't commit petty crimes, not if they want to take care of their reputation.

There are other inconsistencies in Skossyreff's biography as the researchers discovered quite soon. He called himself the Count of Orange and wasn't, and in fact couldn't be anything of the kind, as this title is reserved for members of the Royal Family of the Netherlands. The title of Baron that he used was also false, as his surname cannot be found on the very short list of families that had that title in the Russian Empire. The Russian historian Alexander Kaffka, highly sympathetic to our hero, tried to find his name in the archives of both the Lycée Louis le Grand in Paris and Oxford University's Magdalen College, without success. The same researcher draws our attention to the possible connection between Boris Skossyreff and a member of the British Parliament, Oliver Locker-Lampson, who was the commander of the British military unit sent to help Russia in its fight against Germany in the First World War. It is true that this connection does explain some of Skossyreff's assertions about his high-level British friends, but the fact remains that most of the connections with the European elite Skossyreff boasted about were totally fictitious. The Russian adventurer, accompanied and financed by the ex-wife of the owner of Marmon Motor Car Company of Indianapolis, seems to have come from God knows where, proclaimed a Constitution, adopted a totally new flag, declared war on the Bishop of Urgell and disappeared into the mist. If the whole thing hadn't happened during the summer months, one would be inclined to think it was an Andorran, Carnival-time joke. There is no way of knowing whether the Consell General de les Valls actually ratified the decision to adopt Skossyreff's program to proclaim himself as monarch. They say it did so, twice (why twice?) on the 8th and 10th of July, 1938, both times with a single dissenting voice. However, there are no mentions of either of the votes in the original record book. As legend has it, only one of the members of the Andorran parliament, its maximum authority, the Syndic Pere Torres from Encamp, was against the candidature of Boris Skossyreff as his Royal Highness, the King of Andorra. Faster than the wind Torres headed to La Seu to warn the Bishop and Co-Prince of Andorra of this highly unexpected and undesirable situation. Other sources maintain that Syndic Pere Torres was, in fact, one of the closest friends and collaborators of the Russian, and that the person who explained the situation to the Bishop was another member of the parliament named Cinto.

The newspaper clippings of the period talk of Skossyreff's Constitution and 'royal bulletins' he was believed to publish, but none of these can be found in the Andorran archives. The traces of Boris's presence in the life of Andorran society have been erased so thoroughly that they seem never to have existed. Antoni Morell's novel 'Boris I, King of Andorra' is read and treated as a work of fiction, which, in fact, it is. In the preface, the author tells us that when he started writing it, a lot of people who had taken an active part in Boris's adventure were still alive, but didn't want to talk about it. He had to put all the material together by himself. He kind of had an edge on it though: one of his grandmothers used to know Boris Skossyreff. In my opinion, the author, very intent on depicting his countrymen as hawks and vipers, largely idealised the Russian adventurer in his descriptions.

I was born a Russian. I've never really wanted to be Russian, it just happened. When I was a child, I tried to look for ancestors of other nationalities, in order to prove to myself that deep down, I might be slightly Swedish, a bit Jewish or maybe Tartar. In vain: at least four generations of ethnic Russians, of totally unglamorous peasant descent, stared at me from both sides of the family tree I was drawing up. One of my great-grandfathers was adopted as a child, and he might have been Georgian, but no one knew it for sure, and anyway, he grew up in considerable poverty in a small Russian village the same way as the rest of my known ancestors. As a child, I dreamt of living in a place where more than one language is spoken, maybe Estonia or Ukraine; my mother thought it was a thoroughly weird idea to wish to be bilingual. Now I live in a place where there's nobody monolingual at all, so I can say my childhood dreams have been fulfilled. My daughter speaks a mixture of Catalan, Russian and French, with occasional sparks of Spanish, Portuguese and English. She is also the first Russian in the Santanyes line, the first Andorran in the Grebennikova line and a mixture of two very different cultures. She got what I had wanted for myself... but I can't change and will be what I am till the day I die. I was born in Russia and every Russian in Andorran history is important to me, even when we are talking of someone who called himself a baron without being a baron, claimed to have studied in Oxford and Paris but hadn't and occupied a prominent place on the list of international swindlers prepared by the Netherlands' Central Intelligence Service. It doesn't seem to matter that before meeting the 'American millionairess" willing to sponsor him, he was repeatedly arrested for forging cheques and stealing gold watches. I regularly try to find noble intentions in the text of the

Constitution he'd drafted for the country he jokingly ruled for a couple of weeks.

I can't say I have been in any way successful in this endeavour. The text of the Monarchical Constitution of the Free State of Andorra dated 1934 (not verified by any archival sources) seems as much a product of megalomania as the fact that the recently enthroned Boris I declared a war on the Bishop of Urgell. I can't say how forming a Government of three ministers, two of whom could be foreigners and giving the Prince (that is, himself, Boris I, King of Andorra) the right to dissolve the Parliament (formerly Consell General) was going to aid the country. However, Boris had arrived in Andorra at a time of unrest. A year before his arrival, both co-princes had intervened against the syndics due to their alleged insubordination, called new elections and sent in a group of French gendarmes to restore order. That makes me think that the Andorrans might have used Boris as a weapon to prevent the abuse of power on the part of the co-princes. It's curious to note that Boris Skossyreff founded his claim to the throne on the historic rights of the Duke of Guise who was no relation of his at all, and on the so-called 'need to protect the Spanish inhabitants of Andorra from exploitation for the benefit of France', a kind of goal that could hardly interest any of the Andorrans forming the Consell General. His modernisation ideas came true about half a century later, but weren't necessarily opportune at the time when he voiced them. Though the ideas of liberty of politics, belief and opinion were progressive, who knows what could have happened if Andorra had been converted into a tourist centre and a tax haven, an interesting strategic point between Spain and France, instead of a kind of exotic mountainous desert. Could refugees have passed through the Andorran mountains if the country had become the refuge of the rich and the famous? Wouldn't Andorra have been invaded, conquered and destroyed? I fear the 'new monarchy' could have sold the country to the Nazi Germans, the Russian aristocrats or the British conservatives, whoever offered the highest price.

Though I am delighted to think that the only Russian who left a trace in the history of Andorra tried to promote education and equality, solidarity and sport, I am also relieved he never made it as the King for more than nine days. A Russian adventurer should never be a winner; he can be a survivor and live a hundred years, leaving behind a string of younger wives and lovers, but he shouldn't ever benefit from the deceptions he perpetrates. His life of glamour must be swift and bright.

Friends and adventurers, pay heed to my advice, you shouldn't intervene in the destiny of countries. Places will follow their own star and find a way to get rid of you before you can stand in their path.

The scion of a Scottish greengrocer
Went bravely up Coma Pedrosa.
The wind sneaked up his kilt
showing just how he was built
And the gals all yelled: come closer.

UNIQUE ANDORRA

by Clare Allcard

Andorra? Unique? How, you may wonder, can a diminutive principality of 180sq miles of mountains - much of it only accessible by helicopter or on foot – be called unique?

Well, Andorra just happens to be one of the most idiosyncratic countries on this planet. Take the Head of State for a start.

THE PRINCES

Uniquely, Andorra is the world's only remaining co-principality, a legal status left over from feudal times. This gives the country the singular distinction of being reigned over by two equal, sovereign Princes, one of whom (the President of France) is the only monarch in the world to be elected by ordinary citizens — though not, of course, by the citizens of Andorra, that would be far too humdrum. (He is also the world's only individual to be a monarch and the head of a republic at the same time.) Andorra's other sovereign prince is appointed by the Pope – naturally – who also happens to be head of the world's smallest sovereign state, Vatican City. Since 1278, this second prince has always been the incumbent Bishop of Urgell, living in his palace ten kilometres across the Spanish border in La Seu d'Urgell.

So how come everything is so complicated? Well it all began in 843, when Charlemagne's grandson, Emperor Charles the Bald confirmed the Valls d'Andorra as a feudal domain. For the next 400 years various powerful barons fought over the valleys until, finally, the contestants were reduced to two: the Bishop of Urgell and the Count of Foix. But they in turn were both under the sovereignty of the Kings of Aragon. Though, if this magnificent medieval pledge of allegiance given by the Aragonese subjects to their King is anything to go by, the yoke did not lie too heavily:

"We, who are as good as you, swear to you who are no better than we, to accept you as our king and sovereign lord, provided you observe all our liberties and laws; and if not, not."

On 8th September, 1278, King Pere II of Aragon and Catalonia urged on by the Bishop, became fed up with the constant bickering and signed a *pariatge*, or treaty of equal sharing, of the feudal rights of the Valleys between these two powerful co-princes.

This was arguably the most important document in Andorra's entire history prior to the 1993 written constitution, for it meant that one robust co-prince counterbalanced the other ensuring that, for the next 700 years, tiny Andorra remained neutral and uninvaded during all the conflicts between its towering neighbours.

In World War I, Andorra did sign up with the Allies against Germany. However, as they never actually took up arms, they were accidentally left off the invitation list to the 1919 Treaty of Versailles and so it wasn't until 1958 that peace between the two nations was finally signed.

During the whole of those seven centuries, Andorra's shrewd manipulation of neighbouring power was thrown into jeopardy only once. In 1589, Henri II, Compte de Foix became Henri IV, King of France, and from then on the co-princeship passed automatically down the line of France's kings and queens.

Until the French Revolution.

One can imagine with what horror the revolutionary Napoleon Bonaparte greeted the news that he was also a feudal co-prince of Andorra. Good grief! His whole street cred could be in jeopardy! He promptly renounced the title. Now it was the Andorrans' turn to be horrified. Without France's power to counterbalance Spain's, what chance their continued independence? There was also the little matter of their hard won French trading privileges. They sent a delegation to Paris to beg Napoleon to reconsider.

History tells us that a few years later, Napoleon's ruling ambitions had far outgrown princely little Andorra and his own revolutionary past. By 1804 he had realised that he was so magnificent that only he himself could place the new Imperial crown of France on his head (absolute power corrupts etc). Clearly any idea that accepting Andorra's princely title could in any way taint his legitimacy had long since been forgotten. He withdrew his refusal. And the Andorrans breathed a sigh of relief.

Could it be that President Sarkozy was remembering Bonaparte when, in 2009, he too threatened to abdicate? He was protesting that his Andorran subjects ran their country as a fiscal paradise (tax haven). The ruse worked despite the fact that the Constitution turned out to have no section on abdication. Andorra is no longer quite the fiscal paradise it once was.

Since the signing of the country's first written constitution in 1993, the co-princes continue as joint head of state but the democratically elected Andorran head of government, the *Cap de Govern*, and parliament retain all executive power. In other words the Princes are constitutional monarchs who reign but do not rule.

The Episcopal Co-Prince, living just across the border, visits his subjects quite often. Foreign ambassadors posted to Spain who have Andorra as part of their remit, call on the Bishop in his palace to present their diplomatic credentials. The Presidents of France live a good deal further away, and are a tad busier, but even they usually make a point of visiting their Andorran subjects at least once during their reign.

THE POST

The news was out! 1879 and France had unilaterally assigned Andorra a *French* postal department number. The Andorrans were furious. Surely the thin end of the wedge? Next they'd be annexing the whole country! Demonstrators took to the streets. The French backed down. Today Andorra is the only country in the world with two postal systems run by two different countries - neither of which is the host nation. Until recently it also, uniquely, provided all internal postal deliveries free of charge.

It happened like this. Since the Pharaohs and before, private messengers, often working in relays, transported letters across countries and beyond. In Andorra, during the Pyrenean winter, carrier pigeons were often used over valleys blocked with snow. Then, in 1840, Britain set up the first postal service using pre-paid stamps for delivering letters. The idea caught on. By 1874, with bilateral national agreements by the dozen, Europe's postal services were in chaos. A meeting was called in Switzerland and, with the Treaty of Berne, 22 nations signed up to form only the world's second international organisation: The General Postal Union. (In case you are curious, the first was the Central Commission for Navigation on the Rhine.) Spain and France were among the signatories. The new system was so popular that four years later the Universal Postal Union (UPU) was formed. Today 194 countries belong. But not Andorra. This is because, back in 1878, the running of Andorra's postal system was allocated to Spain. At the time Spain did nothing. Which is when France whirled in to try and fill the vacuum.

It wasn't until 1929 that the Spanish government finally got their act together and issued the world's first stamp with the word 'Andorra' written on it and set in motion a postal service via Spain. The French, now with the agreement of the Andorran government which didn't want to be annexed by Spain anymore than by France, applied to the UPU and were granted equal rights with Spain over Andorra's postal service.

In 1965, Co-Prince President de Gaulle, in an act known as *le compte partage*, decreed that half the French post office's annual profits in Andorra should be returned to the Andorran people. This money is said to have formed the foundation of the country's present social services. However, since 2002, there have been no profits and so nothing to share.

Until the introduction of the euro, one had, most inconveniently, to carry around two purses: one containing

French francs to pay the French post office and another with Spanish pesetas for the Spanish one. (Another quirk of Andorra is that it has never had its own currency.)

Until recently, the two postal systems vied with each other to produce the most decorative stamps possible. Sadly for philatelists, self-adhesive stamps produced digitally and to order in the post offices are slowly superseding the beauties of the past. However, if you ask, new commemorative issues are still to be found in both postal systems.

THE SCHOOLS

My friend Karen arrived in Andorra with one small son to educate and a confusing plethora of choices. Back home it was simple: State or Private. Here, in this strange new land, should she choose the Andorran school to help him integrate into local society and learn the country's official language, Catalan? Or maybe the French school which some said had a better standard at secondary level or even the Spanish? In the end she started him off in the Andorran system.

As you can see, Andorra's education is even more convoluted than its postal service as it has no less than three education systems run by three different sovereign states in three different languages. Not bad for a country with a population of around 75,000!

Education in Andorra is compulsory from 6 to 16. All schools aim to produce children fluent in at least three languages: Catalan, French and Spanish, by the time they are 12. This multi-lingual aspect of Andorra is one of its many charms. The main problem is that, so far, the world's most important international business, IT and medical language, English, runs a poor fourth.

For tertiary education most students go either to France or Spain with a smattering heading for the UK or the USA. Since 1997 Andorra has had its own small university offering degrees in nursing, computing and business studies. Many other courses are offered online.

ANDORRA AND DEMOCRACY

What's so unique about Andorra's democracy? I'll share that with you in just one moment. First let's take a quick whirl through the country's parliamentary history. Andorra's first official efforts at representative government date back to 1419 when the Episcopal Bishop in La Seu granted the country the right to set up the *Consell de la Terra* or Land Council. In those days only the heads of the most important *Cases*/Houses (similar to clans) could be on the council. It wasn't until 1866 that the great *síndic general*, Don Guillem d'Areny Plandolit, introduced the *Nova Reforma.* 523 of the existing 931 Heads of Houses signed the reform, thus enfranchising all Andorra's heads of houses, big and small. But that left out an awful lot of younger brothers – to say nothing of sisters.

Almost 70 years later, in 1933, those disenfranchised young men led Andorra's only political revolution.

On April 10th, 1933 a journalist reported under a subheading 'Universal Suffrage Won': (sic)

"A successful revolution in the world's smallest republic – Andorra – has just taken place. It was bloodless, and the rebels, who were mainly youths, achieved the universal

suffrage which they demanded.

Several motor-cars, driven by young men, went through the villages of Andorra valley, calling out their compatriots to join a demonstration. Five demonstrators formed themselves into a committee, which put their demands before the Council.

The demands were first of all rejected, whereupon the demonstrators rushed the [parliament] building, and renewed their demands for the vote, to which the Council acceded..."

Of course the subheading is incorrect. Andorra did not achieve *universal* suffrage until 1970 when women, too, were given the vote. Which brings us to the unique part of our story.

In the recent parliament, from 2011 to 2015, Andorra became the only country in the world with true gender equality: 14 of their MPs were women and 14 were men. (Rwanda is often awarded top position as it has 63% female members of parliament but then, in my book, that is not gender equality.)

Yesterday, a Sunday, I went to the polls to vote in our local elections. What a wonderful, bustling family scene! In the entrance hall *coca* (sweet cake) and Muscatel were on offer and small children were everywhere. They joined the queue going down to the polling station, some of them still in arms. They went into the voting booths with a parent and then, when they came out, some were given the supreme treat of being lifted up to pop the sealed envelope into the large Perspex ballot box. Voters in training for a democratic future. And today I heard I'd got my man in – with a little help from the other 74% of voters! David Baró, the mayor, had done such an impressive job over the past four years that he actually increased his percentage of the vote this time around.

THE HOSPITAL

The Brit had come out to Andorra on a package skiing holiday. He was well into his 70's and had an artificial hip. But this chap was a goer; a bit of an Eddie the Eagle. He decided to 'have a go' at the snowboarders' half pipe. And, like Eddie, he failed. He ended up in Andorra's hospital with his other hip broken. Which is where the real problems began. Not helped by the side effects of a general anaesthetic, this old boy was seriously confused by the standard of the single, en suite room he woke up in. Maybe he thought his hotel room had been upgraded? Like many Brits missing his fish and chips, he found the hospital fare pretty drear so he decided to look for a more upmarket restaurant. No one saw him leave on his new hip. It was dark outside and snowing. Once his escape was discovered a city-wide police search was launched. He couldn't be found. Until, that is, the following morning when a cleaner found him, fast asleep in an empty room on the first floor of the hospital. Which is when members of the local British community were called in to set up a 24 hour watch over him.

Worried what might happen if *you* have a ski or biking accident whilst on holiday in Andorra? Well don't – worry I mean. One day, in my role as a hospital volunteer, I popped into a room on the trauma ward for a friendly visit. The patient had a badly broken back. But, used to commanding rather than to obeying, she told me she was insisting they fly her home instantly by air-ambulance despite the fact that the doctor had told her that the slightest jolt could leave her paralysed. I pointed out that in the most recent World Health Organisation report, judging the world's health services on a set of five criteria including infant mortality, longevity and citizen's satisfaction with their medical service, Andorra had come third. Britain 15th. I also pointed out that, when having back surgery, you wanted surgeons with lots of practice. I told her that to my certain knowledge the previous year had seen eight broken backs amongst the British skiers alone. She was unlikely to find such expertise in the UK. On cue her anxious doctor bustled in. She held her hand up.

"Don't worry. It's OK! I'm staying. She's persuaded me that it's best to have you operate." I sent up a silent prayer that all would go well – and it did.

When asked by the BBC why he thought Andorrans lived longer than almost any other people on earth, a hospital doctor replied that he thought it was due to genes, altitude, low crime/ low stress – and the fact that you could get a decent glass of red wine in the hospital cafeteria.

So how come such a small country has such a great health service? One of the secrets is that Andorra does not treat all conditions itself. Patients are also helicoptered from the hospital's helipad to first class hospitals in Toulouse, France and Barcelona, Spain. (In that WHO survey France came second and Spain fourth which no doubt boosted Andorra's ratings too.)

All people who are employed in Andorra have to pay into CASS, the national health system. Passive Residents (non-working ex-pats) have to take out private insurance and pay more to use the facilities. There is one, 212 bed hospital. Here all patients have single rooms with en suite bathrooms. Each has a bell to summon staff and individually controlled heating and air-conditioning. Wifi and TV is on offer at a small daily fee. Every room is also equipped with a comfortable couch where, if a patient has recently had surgery, a relative or friend is encouraged to sleep at night so they can warn the nurses if anything is needed. Couples who come out on package deals and have to stay behind because one of them is in hospital often find, at 17€ a night, this is the cheapest sleeping option for the partner. And don't forget there's always that red wine in the cafeteria not to mention a huge terrace with mountain views on which to drink it.

GARBAGE COLLECTION AND ROAD CLEARING

Yes, even garbage collection is pretty special in Andorra. General garbage, plus paper and cardboard for re-cycling, is collected every day, including Christmas, from ubiquitous bin banks while the recycling bins for plastics, containers and glass are emptied twice weekly.

Come the winter there's no need to get out of bed in the dark to see what the road conditions are like. If there's been a fall of snow then you can hear the snowploughs clearing and salt-sprinkling the main roads from 5am and, unless there's been an exceptionally heavy fall, all are clear in time for people to get to work. Those living on minor roads may have to wait a little longer. However, it is not without reason that Andorra has one of the highest per capita number of 4x4 vehicles in Europe. They are needed. In summer other local council vehicles travel along the streets and country lanes cleaning and sweeping them. It is rare indeed to see litter in Andorra.

BROADBAND INTERNET CONNECTIVITY

Another curious point: Andorra, with virtually 100% fibre-optic connectivity, has a far more ubiquitous Internet service than, for instance, the United States. If fluent English could be added to its top notch connectivity, low taxes and impressive quality of life, Andorra could easily become a leading IT hub in Europe

CRIME & THE POLICE

Ask any ex-pat why he or she decided to settle in Andorra and one of the reasons is likely to be "because it's safe". And it is. When, in her early twenties, my blonde and, dare I say it, beautiful daughter worked in Andorra, my only concern when she walked home alone in the small hours of the morning was that someone stoked-up on cheap alcohol might run her over. I myself once left my handbag with credit cards, passport and a handy sum of money on a high street bench. I rushed back for it. But it had already gone. Two hours later the police rang to say a passer-by had handed it in. More recently I accidentally dropped my smartphone in the road at night. I rang a friend the next morning. She chuckled and asked if I realized my mobile had spent the night in police custody? She'd tried to ring me and the police had answered. In case you do lose anything remember there's a central lost and found department at the main police station in Escaldes-Engordany. More than likely it will have been handed in.

Statistically, the country has one of the lowest crime indexes in the developed world. As computed a few years ago by Interpol and based on countrywide data on murder, rape, robbery, aggravated assault, burglary, larceny and motor vehicle theft, Japan's index was 1709.88, Andorra's was not too far above at 1886.37 with the United States standing at 4123.97.

However, beware. The packed streets at Christmas and Easter do sporadically see an influx of pickpockets from Barcelona. Also, when the poorer East European countries were first admitted to the EU, the country was plagued by their extremely amateur thieves (one lot still had all the price tags on the stolen clothes when caught at the border.) Happily they soon learnt that, in a small country with tight borders that can close minutes after a robbery is reported, the chances of being arrested are high. Which has left the locals to relax into tranquility once more.

Andorra depends on neighbouring Spain and France for external defence. The local police force has responsibility for internal security while a comforting number of traffic police remain visible on the streets. Ask one of them the way and they will salute you with old-fashioned courtesy before replying.

One final distinctive aspect of Andorra is the Sometent: all able-bodied Andorran men who own firearms must serve, without remuneration, if called on by their country. From the 18th century onwards all Heads of Household had to have a gun, gunpowder and bullets. Each parish appoints a Captain of Sometent. This civilian militia is unique in a couple of ways: all of its men are treated as officers and the force has not seen any real action for more than 700 years.

It was, however, called out during the great flood of 1982 and, more recently, to help put out forest fires. When Mitterrand, then the President of France and Co-Prince of Andorra, visited his subjects in 1984, the Sometent were on the streets to greet him. Today its main activity is to present the Andorran flag at official ceremonies.

Remember the old Pete Seger song 'Andorra'? The chorus went like this:

I want to go to Andorra, Andorra, Andorra,
I want to go to Andorra, it's a place that I adore,
They spent four dollars and ninety cents
On armaments and their defense,
Did you ever hear of such confidence?
Andorra, hip hurrah!

#1 FESTIVAL

New Year's Eve/Day

Pubs, bars, discos and households all over Andorra and Spain turn their televisions up to welcome in the New Year. This is so as to hear the all-important midnight chimes of the Puerta del Sol clock in Madrid. Stacked on all sides are grapes, nowadays sometimes in special little tins of twelve, otherwise still on the bunch. You select twelve and wait. Sharp at midnight the clock strikes. You gobble the grapes in hectic succession, one for each chime. If you manage to eat them all before the chimes finish then you're assured of a prosperous year ahead! Immediately afterwards everyone raises their glass of cava or champagne to toast in the New Year. But don't look for fireworks. Except for the odd New Year rocket or firecracker there'll be no action.

WINTER

In the night, headlights
fierce on the ski slopes: they are
ironing the snow.

Valerie Rymarenko

THE SKINNY ON SKIING

by Iain Woolward

I'm not a great skier but I've been around, from Aspen to Aviemore… polar opposites in the snowy world of ski resorts. The former, nestled in the Rocky Mountains, accessible only by executive jet and stretch limousine – or so it would appear from the huge toys lined up on both sides of the terminal at the otherwise modest airport. The latter, Aviemore, plonked down on the rolling moorlands of the Scottish Highlands accessed, when last I was there, by a tiny wee road jammed with buses, their windows all fugged up, interiors dank with wet wool. The other distinguishing feature of Aviemore is the scarcity of ski lifts and, more importantly, toilets. The latter wouldn't be an insurmountable problem but for the want of trees to provide privacy when nature screams. While males can at least delve through layers of blizzard-proof clothing in the wide open, groping for and wrestling free the implement with which to sign their names in the snow, for females it is another matter.

For me, the swishiest ski resorts - Aspen, Vail, Chamonix and so on - are just too 'twee'. They offer the skiing experience as imagined by Disney or Universal Studios. Here and there, reality peeks through all that perfection, reminding me of drinking establishments in New Jersey with names like 'Ye Olde (Something-or-Other)', their faux authenticity embossed on their exteriors by Tudor'ish 'wooden' exoskeletons in brown fiberglass, faded to a greyish hue by the smog. The more recently constructed resorts in America are really just theme parks in which 'guests' – at least the ones over thirty – tend to eat, shop, and eat a bit more before flopping into a hot tub after an exhilarating and entirely imaginary 'day on the piste'. To be fair, a lot of them do lug their skis around too, jabbing them inadvertently here and there.

The stodgier European alpine resorts aren't as artificial, given that they invented downhill skiing in the first place. The skiers ski a whole lot harder and the beer mugs come a whole lot bigger... all the better for anaesthetizing you against the grotesque prices. These older resorts have been shaped by almost a century of use. I don't want to appear fixated on toilets (my prostate is just fine, thank you), but if you want to get the measure of how well a ski resort actually works, check out the 'Ladies' at lunch time. As with the great opera houses of Europe, the ladies' toilets are often a nightmare: long lines of anxious-looking women hopping from foot to foot, stuck in architectural bottlenecks that took no account of fashion or physiology.

All of the above leads me to why I like skiing in Andorra: it's probably the most authentic, no-nonsense, well-organized ski resort on the planet. Come winter, the whole country is devoted almost entirely to providing skiers with a good time. The nation depends on it. Sure, the 'après ski' is less shi-shi than you'll find in a Val d'Isere or Klosters. The DJs in Andorra don't make 400,000 euros a year. Not many Andorrans do. But to me that's just fine. The music is good and the crowds manageable. If you don't intend to chat with more than four or five folks over a drink or two, why do you need six hundred party animals between you and the bar?

For the bare facts on Andorran skiing please refer to the section entitled, well, 'Bare Facts'. You'll see that, besides being relatively affordable if you include your hotel, meals and drinks, skiing is also well organized on a quietly industrial scale. Those of you who have shuffled along inch by inch in queues ('lines') at, say, Squaw Valley, California for twenty minutes at *every* lift, and *any* time of day, getting jostled by wide-eyed twenty-somethings reeking of dope, will share my opinion that enjoyable skiing is as much about how you get *up* the slopes as down. In that regard Andorra is almost dreamlike. Yes, it can take a few minutes to hop on a lower lift at rush hour. Thereafter, any momentary queues are quickly spirited away to the comforting, uninterrupted hum of high-speed quads. The lifts at higher altitudes are generally queue-less. And, by the way, illegal substances are treated very vigorously as such in Andorra.

For reasons I'll explain, Andorra is relatively free of the more-than-occasional shoddy conduct of the Type A personalities who flock to swisher resorts and wouldn't be seen dead at such a celeb-light resort as Andorra. You know the sort: pre-programmed with behaviours learned while wiggling obnoxiously through rush hour traffic in Paris on a twice-daily basis or ice-picking their way to the summits of global law firms. They can really take the shine off your day's skiing. On the other hand, purpose-built 'Family' ski resorts (North Star in California, for example) that were created to engender a friendlier tone end up merely reducing the average age of the ill-behaved. But I admit, having passed well-beyond child rearing years, where others see "Aaaww! Soooo CUTE!!" I see tiny pole-less blobs snow-ploughing back and forth across the entire chute, utterly unpredictably. Often they come in continuous and impenetrable strands conducted by a yawning instructor texting his or her evening's date.

One reason that skiers in Andorra seem more relaxed about their day's sport is that most of them come to Andorra from a country that has won but two medals in the history of the Winter Olympics: Spain. These genial people are not aggressive skiers - or, I should add, expert. The Spanish win most of their Olympic medals doing stuff like sailing; they like to have a nice time and have granted themselves, by law, a minimum of twenty two days of paid vacation a year in which to do so.

If you're wondering why Andorrans are not the most prevalent skiers on the slopes of their own country, the answer is: 275:1. That's the ratio by which Andorrans are outnumbered by visitors on any given day. Many come just to gorge on tax-free shopping, many to ski, many to do both. A lot of English people ski in Andorra. I suppose if you like skiing but live in one of the flattest, rainiest nations on earth you'll be naturally drawn to the sunniest, most mountainous country in Europe: Andorra has more pistes as a percentage of its total area than anywhere in the world and the odds are over 80% that the sun will shine the day you choose to ski down them. Admittedly, the English are crap skiers. No English person has ever come even close to medalling on skis of any kind, at any time. (A laddie from neighbouring Scotland won a slalom skiing Olympic medal once, but he had to give it back because he'd smeared a well-known brand of chest rub on himself before the event). However, the English seem well aware of their ineptitude in slippery conditions. They are politely cautious in a non-Latin way on the slopes and they do queue really well. Barging is profoundly shunned in England and where the English gather.

And so it seems to me that people have more *fun* skiing in Andorra than elsewhere. It's all a bit of a laugh. I have not a shred of scientific evidence to support this notion. And it could be that I'm still overly influenced by my initial impression of the place. On the first ride I ever took on an Andorran chairlift I sat next to a young guy who, sensing I wasn't local, enquired in French if I spoke any. The French in which I answered told him I didn't.

"English?"

"Scottish," said I.

My companion immediately broke into a dead ringer of a Glaswegian accent, "Do yees ken any jokes aboot skiing in Scoootland? - other than the skiing itself, of course!!" A perfectly enunciated perfect example of self-effacing Scottish humour: funny because it's true. Smiling, I asked him where he'd skied in Scotland.

"Aaa've neverr even bin therre!!" Turned out he was French, living and working in Brussels; spoke four languages, three in multiple dialects. The enforced intimacy of chair lifts was the perfect place for him to practice them.

It's hard to get a good laugh like that on a ski lift in Vail or Klosters.

Now, about the actual *skiing* in Andorra: if your skis are over 200 cms long and skinny enough to pick teeth, or you have more than one set of them, it's probable that neither I nor Andorra have a great deal to offer you. Yes, I've skied in more places than most, but never well. And, yes, Andorra does host world-class alpine ski events on long, challenging runs, but most of the skiing is 'intermediate'. You'll be pressed to find an undressed mogul, let alone fields of them. Regarding powder: as you may know, when ski resorts boast "XX% Powder Days!!!", what they're also saying is that, for nearly XX% of the time, you'll be skiing in a blizzard. Most of the rest of the time it'll be cloudy and cold to preserve powder conditions.

If you crave carving through waist-high powder until your thighs feel like they're burning in the fires of hell, Andorra may disappoint. It's the second southern-most ski resort in Europe. Furthermore, most of Andorra's slopes are exposed to afternoon sun. More sun, less powder or ice. Also, given the intermediate skier market to which Andorra appeals, resort staff work through the night to dress and re-dress vast swaths of mountainside, leaving not a whole lot of easily-accessible virgin stuff. Also, most Andorran runs, especially on the north-western, arguably more scenic, side of the country are shorter than those to be found in most Alpine resorts. Andorra is more akin to the bowl skiing of the Sierra Nevada of California. My view is that, if you like to adjust your boots such that you can still feel your feet, or if you've been known to pull up on long runs pretending to adjust them (your boots, that is), Andorran runs are ample and nicely varied, to boot.

The 'Bare Facts' should tell you everything else you need to know. Come skiing in Andorra. You'll have fun.

SKIING IN ANDORRA: THE BARE FACTS

The two ski areas (Grandvalira & Vallnord) comprise:

300 kms of groomed piste

187 runs (37 Green; 63 Blue; 56 Red; 31 Black)

Over 3,000 hectares/7,500 acres of skiable area

Up to 1010 meters of vertical drop

109 lifts capable of handling 159,465 skiers per hour

Snow-making equipment guarantees skiing on at least 50% of the runs

3 Ski Schools: over 500 instructors

Over 50 restaurants

Wide variety of degrees of difficulty: world cup courses to 'family' skiing

#2. FESTIVAL

5th/6th January. Twelfth Night/ Epiphany/ Three Kings/ Reis

Long before Andorra's children had heard of Father Christmas they cannily delivered their wishes to the Pages of the Three Kings, those Wise Men who travelled from afar bearing gifts of gold, frankincense, and myrrh.

Today, on the evening of 5th January, seven trios of Kings, or *Reis,* ride into their seven respective towns, clad in regal finery: gold crowns, velvet cloaks, flowing locks and splendid false beards. They progress down the main streets of Andorra La Vella, Escaldes and Encamp on theme-decorated floats sometimes accompanied by elves. In La Massana the men of the Orient usually arrive in a clattering horseback cavalcade whilst Pas de la Casa transports their Reis aboard 4x4s! The public throng the streets. Small children rush forward to scoop up the literally hundreds of kilos of sweets that the Kings throw to the crowd. Next morning those same children will find that the Kings, bearing gifts, have visited them in the silence of the night.

There's also a Three Kings' Cake (most festivals worth their salt in Andorra have a distinctive cake.) This one, *Tortell de Reis* is decorated with green, orange and red crystallized fruits, filled with marzipan or custard and topped off by a golden crown. Each cake is baked complete with a tiny china figurine of a *Rei* and also a dried broad bean hidden inside. Win the *Rei* and you're king for the day and get to wear the crown. End up with the bean and you pay for the *tortell* – and possibly have a broken tooth thrown in.

A WINTER'S TALE

by J. P. Wood

Turn back fifty years, or so.

Winter falls on the small country of Andorra like a harsh enchantment. From October till March, the children trek to school, hard work enough through the deep snows and ice, but not so hard as their spring and summer labours guarding the flocks on the summer pastures or taking food to their fathers where they labour in the stony fields; fields which will now lie fallow until the snows melt, in March, or perhaps even April.

A numb tranquillity falls over the stone villages couched down beneath the ramparts of the Pyrenees. Come the long nights, families sit around the fire, women knitting, sewing, men mending, repairing, occasionally venturing out to see if the beasts in the barns and byres are safe. Children sit on the floor by the fire, conning their books, scuffling, giggling, while the cat, relieved from mouse-duty, sits scratching for fleas.

It is the time for boasting or lamenting over the harvest, the time when old stories and legends do the rounds, and when the children talk and talk and talk of the cornucopia of feast days to come.

There is Purissima, feast of the Immaculate Conception, precursor of the first heavy snowfalls, then the Christmas Eve Vigil with the snowy trek to midnight mass, and afterwards, outside the candle-lit church, a gorging on hot chocolate and the sweet cake, *coca*; next the Holy day of the Nativity, followed by the feast of the good Saint Esteve (Steven), after whom so many Catalan boys are named; and finally that most blissful day, Epiphany, when the three Kings bring gifts to good children. Tailing after Christmas comes the Feast of the Innocents, traditional time of jokes and tricks, and before you can blink it is time for Carnival and the long austerities of Lent.

All these the children talk of in excited whispers, but suddenly they break into raucous laughter, the adults look on with indulgent smiles and the teenage girls wrinkle their noses and make exaggerated noises of disgust. An unbridled, less holy spirit has entered the room as every mind turns to a more pagan day.

It is nearly time say the men, and the women nod agreement. It is time for the *Matança del Porc,* the Slaughter of the Pig, for does the old song not say, '*Per Nadal posarem el porc amb sal*'. 'For Christmas we will salt the pig'.

So, before the pigs become scrawny on their winter diet, *el gross,* the big one, will be brought forth from the barn, yelling his head off, and he will be sacrificed with all the ancient and bloody ceremony.

Yes, yes, I hear you say. That was **Then**, this is **Now**, and many, many things have changed. And of course, my friend, you are quite right. Now, tourism and commerce are the new crops, an all year labour with no fallow time. Few now farm this harsh and stony land for their living, except for tobacco and the exquisite Andorran potato. Today, the children follow normal term times, probably to their everlasting regret, and the centre of the long winter night is the one-eyed god, the flickering telly.

However, the holy feast days are still celebrated. There is a shade more commerce to them, but they are nonetheless times of family joy; and still the children giggle and shriek in anticipation of the *Matança del Porc.* Yes! The tradition continues, not on quite such a scale as in the days when every household that could, slaughtered the pig to ensure food for all the family during the winter months. There is too, perhaps less horse-play and daubing with blood, and I do not believe that these days menstruating women are forbidden to take part in the making of *botifarres,* (sausages). Rarely now is the pig home-reared, but is brought in a trailer from some country market, kept perhaps a week or two to be fattened.

Today, his time has come.

The farm-yard, or until quite recently, the pavement outside the house or flat, is swept and scrubbed by a teenage girl who still wrinkles her fastidious nose in disgust. Trestles are put out, straw is scattered thickly by grinning, yelling brats. Families, friends, often the entire village, gather, stamping their feet, for the sun has not yet reached the sacrificial altar and the frost glitters. Someone, a lady or maiden of the house, may bring out hot chocolate. The men have probably tucked a couple of coffees and brandies under their belts; those, and anticipation, lend a sparkle to their eyes and a liveliness to their voices.

A moment of silence: the trailer door is opened, the occupant peers beady-eyed and fearful into the day to be cajoled, poked and prodded until he makes **his** entrance onto **his** stage where he will play **his** last, most gallant role before a most enthusiastic audience.

Silence is broken as eager hands reach out to lift the pig onto the trestle, his snorts and anxious shrieks surprisingly effete. The children jostle and shove for the honour of holding a thrusting porcine leg, the men add their weight to the now arching torso, while women look round to make sure a bucket is to hand, to make sure the smallest tot hasn't got its head too near one of those sharp little trotters. The village maidens cover their faces, but cast slanting glances through their fingers as the chosen one, usually a man, approaches the victim, his face solemn, the blade of his trusty, well-honed, well-used knife held lightly in one hand.

The knife arcs, the pig shrieks, and shrieks for if the meat is to be good, he must bleed to death. A jet of blood, redder than red and seemingly everlasting, flows into the bucket while the faces watching its death throes are rapt in the way that their ancestors' faces were rapt.

Then the pig is still; the laughter and chatter start again while the men heap the body with straw to burn off the bristles and the children boast of how it was the biggest strongest pig ever, and how they personally had held it down. A pallid maiden is packed off to make more coffee.

The rest is a *festa,* a party; a hard-working, pig-dismembering, sausage-making, eating and drinking party that will continue into the small hours until the last morsel of pig has been butchered, hung, ground, or rendered into joints, brawn, sausages, lard, every little bit, including the ears, stored for use. Since these days professional butchers are less in use, there is no one to cart off an ear, the snout, or other chosen delicacies in payment for services rendered.

The food produced by the *Mestressa,* the lady of the house, to sustain her eager workers, may include traditional dishes of *pasta soup,* rabbit and rice, cabbage or perhaps curly endive picked from beneath the snow. One thing is for sure, the meal will be washed down with wine, beer and brandy.

All this time, the one-eyed god sits neglected and unworshipped in its corner, the fat Range-Rover in the garage is forgotten, so too is the supermarket with its accessible bounty of shrouded joints. Instead, the revellers are filled with an old and cheerful consciousness of a full larder and that, in this harsh and cruel winter, the apocalyptic demon, hunger, will once more be kept at bay.

Next morning, I look out at the still closed shutters behind which my neighbours sleep off their bacchanalia and I see shreds of bloodied straw blowing in the wind, an empty bottle rolling down the street, and there, on the abandoned trestle, a last row of fat pink sausages glistening in the frosty morning light.

The Pyrenean range is quite old
'Lower Cretaceous', so I am told.
France crashed into Spain
Again and again
Forcing the border to crumple and fold.

#3 FESTIVAL

17TH January: The Feast of Sant Antoni and the Pig/The Day of the Free Lunch.

First comes the *Encants*. In times gone by, when the ground was hard with frost, every Andorran family that could afford it would butcher a pig to keep them in meat through the winter. Traditionally, on Sant Antoni, people donated pieces of their butchered pork: ears, trotters, hams, chops, sausages to be auctioned for charity. The rich were expected to bid way above the odds for things that they themselves may have donated. Today the tradition is alive and well. In 2014 the *Encants* of Escaldes-Engordany alone raised 7,560€. In the past the money went to the local priest. Today it usually goes to the charity, Caritas, which, amongst other things, runs Andorra's food bank.

Escudella, a hearty meat-rich stew, follows. It will probably contain chicken, pork, pork sausages and slices of large meat balls all cooked up with carrots, leeks, celery, potatoes, dry beans and noodles. And who said there's no such thing as a Free Lunch? The parishes' main squares sprout trestle tables topped with *porrons* of red wine whilst huge cauldrons, fuelled by stacks of firewood and stirred by men and women in traditional costume, brew up the stew. Being free, the queues are long so come warmly clad. Bring your soup bowl and spoon or buy one of the attractive commemorative earthenware bowls produced each year by the Comuns to help defray the actual cost of the 'free' meal. Some people have complete bowl collections dating back years.

THE GREAT ANDORRAN AVALANCHE

by Clare Allcard

Tuesday, 8th February, 1996. For days now snow had been falling from sullen skies. In the tiny ski resort of Arinsal it stood piled high at the sides of the road. The operators had closed the slopes to the public whilst employees laboured with shovels to free the main chairlift from the previous night's heavy fall. With visibility down to 200 metres, Hugh Garner, the English resort manager for Arinsal, rang round the ski reps warning them not to send up their coach-loads of clients. From the roof of Arinsal's diminutive Hotel Micolau strange, metre high crests of snow froze, melted, slipped and froze again, curling over the roof's edge like the petrified spume of white breakers.

At approximately 10.50am, a wild boar, pushing its way under a pine tree's laden branches, set off the Percanela avalanche. Swooping down the narrow, Percanela gully, it careered across the Arinsal road depositing some two meters of snow and debris between the Sant Andreu Aparthotel to the south and the Amadeus building above to the north, and finally ending up in the river, effectively cleaving the village in two. Above the avalanche, near the ski station and the bars, it left some five hundred people stranded.

The mayor, Antoni Garrallà, remained seriously concerned. Huge quantities of unstable snow still hung in the vast natural bowl of mountain high up beyond the village. They had had one small avalanche but could there perhaps be another, much bigger one, waiting to happen? At around

11.20am, after consultation with various government ministers and senior police and fire officers, Garrallà took the initiative and ordered the whole area above the Percanela avalanche to be evacuated. Garner told me later that, at first, he thought the Mayor must be joking; that he couldn't possibly mean evacuate the whole area: the hotels, the apartment blocks, the studio flats, shops and bars - but he did.

Calling in helpers, they split into teams, one for each staircase in each building with one policeman, one fireman and one English-speaker assigned to each team. (With the resort particularly popular with the British, some 90 per cent of the evacuees were expected to be English-speaking.)

The orders were clear: ring at the front door of every single flat and, if after ringing and knocking, no one answered, break down the door. Those teams of men ended up breaking down dozens of doors. They scoured every single room in every single building checking for inhabitants.

They told all occupants they encountered to leave at once taking with them as many essentials as they could carry.

At the Percanela avalanche itself the rescue services and ski instructors, armed with two-metre long snow poles, stood shoulder to shoulder in a long line, shoving the poles downwards through the hard compacted snow, trying to sense the squishy feeling that might indicate a possible body or survivor. Happily they found none.

The evacuation of the four Prats Sobirans apartment blocks further up the valley proved more complicated. Luckily - or unluckily depending on your point of view - Hugh had a mini-van trapped above the Percanela. He sent it up four times to carry people away from the buildings.

Police, firemen, local council employees and even snow-plough drivers guided the many evacuees: shop keepers, ski instructors and chairlift operators as well as residents and tourists, either over the avalanche and down to the lower village or else through the vast, half-finished apartment block just below the ski lift. This building had its pros and cons. Its advantage was that, at its base, it led out onto the road below the Percanela avalanche. The cons were that, unfinished as it was and with no outer walls, it was icy cold inside. To add to the fun, it also lacked sufficient stairways to connect one floor to the next! Rescuers had hastily to erect rickety, home-made ladders where needed and, all along the route, the rescue services gently coaxed people to climb always downwards until, from the basement, they reached a bridge across the Valira River to safety.

Many have sung those helpers' praises.

Just below the Sant Andreu Aparthotel the police stationed two manned, 4x4s to prevent anyone returning up the valley. Earlier in the day, the avalanche committee requisitioned the lounge of the Sant Andreu as their main co-ordination centre.

Meanwhile, in the Hotel Micolau, the hotelier Fiona Dean reported strange happenings. The gas wouldn't light in the kitchen. Lavatories wouldn't flush. The clichés, too, were all in place: an eerie silence, not even a dog barking, a thick deadness to the air, an oppressive sense of impending doom, of the world holding its breath in prelude to a cataclysmic disaster.

At 4pm, the evacuation teams, totally exhausted, reported back to the Sant Andreu. All the buildings were now empty.

An hour later one of the biggest avalanches ever recorded in the Pyrenees, spewed downwards to fill the valley and the river with debris so that, days later, one could still walk on its back from one side of the valley to the other, a huge plain of snow varying from 10 to 20 meters (32 – 65 feet) in depth.

Les Fonts was a dry snow avalanche, the spectacular kind where a beautiful, fluffy powder cloud of air and snow travels just above the main avalanche and moves faster than the debris beneath it. This cloud can reach up to 200 kph or the speed of a major hurricane.

More dangerous still, just in front of the powder cloud hurtles an invisible front wind or 'air blast'. If caught in its full embrace, it can explode a person's lungs.

Starting much higher up the mountain than Percanela, by the time Les Fonts charged into the Peu de Pistes building, it stretched 500 metres wide. The huge velocity of the air blast hit the building's ground floor and then exploded heavenwards. Whole trees, like great battering rams, were propelled through the windows and forced ever upwards through the floors above until the front wind actually blew off the building's roof, blasting it further up the mountainside and leaving tree trunks packed, tight as a timber yard, within.

And then it stopped; set hard as concrete – a curious feature of avalanche snow. (The violence inside the avalanche grinds the large, feathery flakes into smaller and smaller particles forming denser and denser snow. Combine this with the heat generated by the avalanche's motion and microscopic droplets of water take shape around each minute speck of ice causing it and the debris to set solid the moment it stops. Victims caught within it will set solid too.)

Les Fonts, when it finally came to rest, had blocked both the ground and 1st floor of the Peu de Pistes with rock-hard snow. 15 months passed before the "concrete" ice began to thaw at the back of the Pic Negre ski shop to reveal a bizarre sight. Interleaved like so many book marks wedged between pages, the ice still stood packed solid between every garment on the clothes rail.

The main car and coach park was entirely buried. Luckily, due to the earlier, poor weather conditions, it harboured only a few dozen cars, all wrecked, including Hugh's mini-van, crushed beneath the weight of snow. One red Fiat mini-bus even ended up wrapped around a pylon.

Lower down in the village, Fiona Dean reported that, "The hotel was jam-packed. I was outside with a friend who had very long hair. There was a moment of complete silence and then, in the very next instant, there was this tremendous roar on top of you. No rumbling in the distance. It was right there. For a second I thought it was a hurricane, then an earthquake. Everything shook so much. But it was the front wind travelling fast as the speed of light before the second avalanche. One moment nothing. A split second afterwards you're being dragged along the street. I remember vividly my friend's hair. The wind lifted it straight up in the air!"

"How did you breathe?" I asked.

"Oh, you mustn't breathe! The front wind, bitterly cold,

forms ice crystals in your lungs and you can drown. No! No! Don't breathe!"

She described how the blast brought with it an onslaught of flying 'stuff'. And not just itsy-bitsy 'stuff' like pine needles but shards of masonry ripped off buildings: parts of chimneys, gutters, skimming roof tiles, anything that the wind could grab and hurl onwards. Standing in front of her hotel, Fiona watched, mesmerised, as the blast scooped up a small van, turned it around in mid-air and then banged it down on its wing. It also picked up one of the police vehicles stopped outside the Sant Andreu, complete with officers inside, and carried them some 100 metres down the road depositing two very shaken policemen a little above Hotel Arinsal.

Antoni Garrallà, coming into the village just after the powder cloud had passed through, said that his lasting impression was of houses' walls, doors and windows, snow-blasted white like a glittering Christmas card.

With everyone evacuated and the road closed, it wasn't until the following morning that people discovered the true extent of the destruction. Hugh Garner, going up with government officials and press to assess the damage, described what he saw. "It was a scene of absolute devastation. And there was this one abiding, over-arching sensation: the smell of resin. Some 10,000 trees smashed to smithereens. Astonishing! No road, no river, no bridge, no cars, just broken trees and snow turned hard as rock. And to show the incredible forces at work, the air blast had ripped a crash barrier clean off its mountings and plastered it across the Peu building where an impression of the stone wall behind had gone right through the metal and embossed itself on the outside!"

According to one of Andorra's main hauliers, it would have needed a convoy of trucks stretching nose to tail, 200 kilometres, (120 miles) from Andorra to Barcelona to clear all the snow away. And, according to a French expert, such an avalanche happens about once every 100 years in the Pyrenees.

It could have been much worse. Only 45% of the unstable snow in the bowl of Les Fonts came down in the avalanche.

At the St Gothard Hotel in Erts, the next hamlet down the road from Arinsal, the evacuees' ordeal was still not over. Hugh formed part of a committee set up to find overnight accommodation for some 300 temporarily homeless people; not easy during the ski season.

In the Micolau, Fiona looked at the crowd of refugees packed into her tiny restaurant and asked "Who has *definitely* got nowhere else to go?" Some 60 people raised their hands! Assuming that help would soon arrive, she and her co-owner, Carol Phillips-Jones bundled people temporarily into rooms already occupied by paying guests. They cleared space on the restaurant floor, phoned round friends in search of extra blankets and put mattresses in the stock room and along the corridors.

"It brought out the best and the worst in people. I got no sleep for three days. It was like being marauded by pirates! Had to keep a constant eye on the stock room to make sure the contents weren't 'liberated'. We were getting desperate. Everyone was dirty, highly strung and exhausted."

The paying customers soon left in search of peace and a good night's sleep whilst the destitute stayed on. For many had not been in their apartments at the time of the evacuation, had not been able to grab their passports, credit cards, wallets and spare clothing. They had been left with nothing but what they stood up in.

And still no help arrived. Meanwhile the police cordoned off the only road leading into the village to prevent looting and possible injuries.

"It was like living in a nuclear contamination zone." said Fiona. "I tried ringing Andorra's British Honorary Consul telling him we desperately needed help. I had 60 people crammed into my 14 bedroomed hotel. He was supposed to be our conduit to the British Consulate in Barcelona. I got no response. In the end I rang my father in Scotland and asked him to contact Barcelona. In those days, nineteen years ago, the Consulate had no idea at all what was going on in this country. They were horrified when they discovered that there were on average, 8,500 Brits here during 16 to 18 weeks each year." She paused. "Things have changed a lot since then!"

For the next three days Fiona and Carol ran a free dosshouse and soup kitchen, mainly great cauldrons of the local escudella stew. They allowed young Argentinean ski instructors, left with nothing, to ring home to reassure their parents and ask for money. The British ex-pat community rallied round. Friends from further afield got permission to come through the cordon to help with the cooking and to take the young down town to buy them wash things and underwear. Carol and Fiona set up a food bank for those who had found alternative accommodation but had no money to buy victuals. Tins of meat, fruit and vegetables arrived along with pasta and rice and bread. Donated second-hand clothes had, in the end, to be turned away as the pile grew so high it blocked the light coming in through the low restaurant windows.

So why did the world hear so little about the Great Andorran Avalanche of 1996? Firstly because, thanks to Antoni Garrallà's initiative, not a single life was lost – except for that of the wild boar. And secondly because, very soon, the world transferred its eyes elsewhere. 27 hours after Andorra's casualty-free avalanche, IRA terrorists blew up London's Canary Warf.

A week later I went up to take a look. I'll never forget driving along a narrow trench dug between towering white walls and then being faced by a massive barricade of ripped up tree trunks embedded in snow. It must have been at least 8 metres (26 feet) high as it totally dwarfed a man standing in front of it.

Less than two weeks after the avalanches, Arinsal ski station re-opened. They had dug a road right through to the ski lift and cleared away wrecked cars. On close inspection experts found that the Peu de Pistes building, solid and simple as it was and housing shops, a bar and flats above, had not budged one inch during the onslaught. Kitted out with a new roof, it rose, phoenix-like to become the renamed Patagonia. The Crest Hotel mainly suffered broken windows whilst the Amadeus, built into the hillside and designed to resist avalanches, did just that. Les Fonts flowed right over the top of its roofs. Not so the four apartment blocks of Prats Sobirans. It blew out windows and crashed into walls and in the end the top two storeys of one block had to be demolished, though not without much argument about compensation.

With the story not making it into the British press, the avalanche barely touched Arinsal's popularity as a ski resort.

For a full, panoramic view of the avalanche site, drive up the road above Arinsal's four-man chair lift to the ski station's upper car park and look across the valley. High up and slightly to the left is the huge bowl that spewed out Les Fonts and to the right the much slimmer gully from where the Percanela raced down. And then, much lower, you can also see the massive avalanche barrier installed to protect the village from any future onslaughts.

Today, if you hear a muffled explosion as you lie in bed of a winter's morning or sip your first cup of coffee in your hotel restaurant, don't panic. It's not a revolution but GAZEX, a remote, computer-operated system today used around the world to detect and safely detonate small avalanches before they become big ones.

> *Ploughmen of Andorra have no fear*
> *At the first sign of snow they appear*
> *Fall as hard as it might,*
> *Snowing all through the night*
> *By morning the streets are all clear.*

THE PIGS ARE NOT IN MOURNING

FICTION

by J. P. Wood

His ears felt so enormous and red, Cris was surprised no one had noticed, or noticed that his feet in their pinching, church-going shoes had gone off to belong to someone else. It was even colder, he thought, than the day they'd gone skiing in a blizzard, the time when Pere's ears had turned chewing-gum grey and the teacher, all tearful, rushed them down the mountain into the cafe, bought them hot chocolate and doughnuts, and hadn't scolded, however much noise they made.

Perhaps he was a sun-lover at heart, like Mama sitting next to him, chin sunk into the collar of her new black coat, pretty face bent over her missal, as white and solemn as one of the angels on the walls; but for all she stared and stared at the print, she didn't join in the responses.

Queer she was so sad. She'd never liked Gramps. With the old man she was most likely to lapse into French instead of Catalan, or even, when she really wanted to provoke, call Cris 'Christophe'. Then the old man would yell that his grandson was called Cristòfol and was a good Andorran boy, not a little French ponce.

His mother would stalk out of the room, muttering about rude old peasants.

Gramps would have liked this weather. He could hear his rough voice. 'Good Saint Anthony's weather. Just right for slaughtering the pigs, Cris boy.'

Closing his eyes to the black backs in front, well salted with dandruff, Cris conjured up last year's Saint Anthony's; the day after his seventh birthday, the age of reason; so the priest said during their First Communion classes. It'd been cold and grey like today, shocking red blood, the sugary stink of the butchered meat, and Marta shrieking and peering through her fingers. Girls, he'd whispered to Uncle Gerard, didn't seem to like the pig-killing much. His uncle looked thoughtful, said he'd noticed girls quite often didn't like the good things of life, but neither of them mentioned Cris's Mama who still hadn't come down to the yard. Finally she'd appeared in an enormous pinny and helped the women stir the dark cauldrons of meat and force the sausages through the growling machine, while all the time her expression declared she really wasn't there.

Grandma was different. She'd no time for mimsy-pimsying around. She could remember years when there hadn't been a pig to slaughter.

The party after the slaughter had been almost as good as Christmas; there was so much to eat. Gramps had still been big and strong, all the family and friends were there and his mother, so pretty, changed into her blue silk dress with the skirt which went shhh-shhh as she danced. She'd danced a lot, not with his father who'd been seriously overseeing the food but with Uncle Gerard and blissfully, once with him, and her perfume had tickled his nose as she whispered into his ear that he was her best little boy.

'Best, Solange?' She'd let him go and turned to Uncle Gerard. 'Little,' she'd repeated, and Gerard, grinning, had said, 'That's all right then,' and had shoved Cris gently away and put his arms round Mama's waist.

Then Gramps had called her over and muttered something into her ear which was when she'd yelled at him. 'Well, you'd like to, old goat.' Everyone had gone all stiff and strange; his father had taken his mother's arm, even though she'd tried to yank it away, and eased her out of the big barn cleared for the feast; then the man with the accordion had struck up loudly and rolled his eyes, while Marta dragged Cris onto the floor and danced with him until he was dizzy and silly, which was nice but queer, because his cousin Marta was five years older and usually pretended he didn't exist.

Opening his eyes, Cris was disappointed to find that the salt on his cracked lips was the salt of his own blood, not chitterlings. No party this year. They were in mourning, which it seemed meant being very, very sad because Gramps was dead; so sad that they couldn't slaughter the pigs; couldn't have a fiesta.

'It wouldn't be proper,' Grandma had said. 'D'you hear now,' she'd repeated to Uncle Gerard, who'd sighed and said, 'Of course Mama, of course.'

And he was almost glad, thought Cris, shifting to the edge of the bench and noticing with surprise that after all his feet were still there. He kicked hard against the stone slabs, and felt a little tingle. Hello, feet.

The first time he'd seen the pigs had been just after coming back from the beach last summer. After all the rows and rackets between Mama and Papa, and then Papa and Uncle Gerard, while Aunt Fina looked on, yellower and more pinched by the day, it had been lovely to stand in the silent, stinky dark and look at the nice piggy faces and scrawny bodies. He'd christened them Nigra, the one with the black face, and Blanca, the one almost as pale as the sausages she was destined to become.

'Hardly original,' his mother had said.

Grandma let him feed them. Goodness, they were fat now, and they snuffled wetly at his hands when he came to give them their swill. While they were eating, he'd scratch their backs, hairy as doormats, and rub their cool, delicate ears. Once, Uncle Gerard passing had laughed and said; 'Delicious,' and Cris, recalling the gritty saltiness of fried pigs' ears, had been sick. And the pigs had gobbled it up with the same relish they took their swill.

So although he was sad about Gramps, he was happy for the pigs who would find pig husbands and have pig babies, and he'd be allowed to adopt one which would follow him everywhere.

Looking up at his mother, he thought maybe not. He wanted to hold her hand, but her hands were not available, they were stroking slowly up and down the front of her black coat, a funny new gesture of hers. She looked down at him gravely, and murmured, 'Cris, be still.'

For a second his mother's hands stopped that stroking which was slow, but not soothing, and he poked one finger out and touched a gloved hand gently, so gently that if she wanted she could ignore it. She raised her face, but did not look at him; instead she gazed across at his father in the front pew, his shoulders stooped as if he still carried the glossy, long coffin, together with Uncle Gerard and other men from the village.

'Mama,' Cris had whispered as the coffin was borne by. 'What's in there?' And she'd looked at him angrily and muttered, 'Why Cris, you know.'

Which he did and he didn't, because there was no way the narrow box, glossy as a conker, handles glittering, the sharp beautiful lines of the cross notching its lid, could ever contain his rough, huge, red-faced old Gramps. Why a few minutes in there, and he'd be out, looking round with his flashing white smile. Lovely teeth his Gramps had. Sometimes when Cris came to say goodnight, he'd let him hold the gnashers in his hands, open and close them, clack, clack, and they'd been damp and hard on his palm. Oh, how Mama had shrieked when she'd come in on them one night. 'Disgusting,' she'd yelled. 'You are truly disgusting.' And the old man had grinned at her, pinkly, and nodded his head like one of those dogs you see in the back of cars. Mama had bounced out of the room.

'Stop fidgeting, Christophe,' she said again from under the hat which swamped hair as bright as his own. And he stopped because when she got very French, she was really cross. She was the only lady in church in a hat. Marta, leaning against Uncle Gerard, showed her brown hair; the others wore scarves or veils, although outside the church, people wore hats galore, but not hats like his mother's, a grand, strange black thing that made her look foreign and distant like the stiff ladies on the church walls. No, those outside hats were jolly, everyday things. Angelina, the cow-girl, wore her red, man's cap. As they'd approached the church, the chatting crowd opening up to let them past, she'd been there, glowing from hat to scarlet boots. He'd longed to run up to her, to push and shove her into whirling him around until the sky and the church span. But she'd shaken her head at him, and he'd followed his mother into the church, too tiny to allow any but the family inside.

'Like a party,' his mother muttered as they moved into the musty gloom. 'That's all it is to them. Wait till the coffin comes past, then they'll think a bit.'

What would they think of, wondered Cris, doing a tiny jig, so tiny surely no one could notice, in time to the swing of the censers and the flicker of candles across the wall where his very own saint, Saint Cristòfol seemed to dance across the river, joggling and bouncing the Christ-child on his shoulder, while the little fishes nibbling at his ankles seemed to joggle and bounce as well.

'God help us! Won't the child be still?' Under his mother's glare, the painted figures, so rich and fine since the men from Barcelona had come with their restoring brushes, became still again. 'What is it?'

He swung his foot faster above the stone flags, and avoided those blue eyes so like the ones which stared out at him from the mirror. 'Just like me,' his mother said when she scrubbed him in the bath. 'All except your hands. Peasant hands you have, from your father.' Then sometimes she'd tell him about France, the south with its sweet scents and great history and her parents' big farm they'd had to sell. Then she'd stop and sigh, and mutter how different it was here. Then depending on her mood, she'd grab him up in a towel and call him her dear little Frenchman, or she'd drop into a long silence, leaving him to sit patiently until the bath-water was cold.

Now, as he slid down from the hard bench, she whispered, 'All right, but be quick.'

Outside, the sky heaved like stew in a pot. Drawing in a deep breath, he snuffled snowflakes and sneezed. The people were still there, most of them gay in their ski clothes, but their faces grown grey like the sky. Angelina took a step towards him and skidded on snow compacted under her feet.

'Fuck!' She grinned at him cheerfully, and then swallowed her grin. 'Why you come out, Cris. It's not respectful to your Gramps.

'I've got to.' He did his little jig. 'Mama said.'

'You want me to keep watch.'

'Please Angelina.'

Behind the cemetery which stuck out from the little church like an awkward tail, he hesitated, and Gramps' old mutt came slinking out of the bushes.

'Doggis, Doggis.' He stretched out his hand but the mutt stood back hooping its bony spine, looking up from filmy eyes.

'Heaven's sake Cris. They'll be doing the committal soon.'

'I can't.' He stared at the crowd, so big it had spread around the whole church.

'Up there.' She nodded to the angle of the wrought iron gate to the cemetery. 'Now turn your back. I'll stand behind. No one will see.'

He watched the steam rise from the pretty gold arc. Then giving himself a little shake, as taught by Uncle Gerard, he looked up and through the gates to the grey, knobbly wall, very old they said, with its deep recesses and the little enamelled plaques. And he stopped shaking and wondered at the square that gaped open, its darkness quite deep enough to swallow up the conker-bright box. Snowflakes drifted across the dark space.

'Is that where they'll put Gramps?'

'What?' Brown eyes crinkled into red cheeks and she gave him a bright smile which made him think of Gramps although he knew her teeth were real. 'Yes. And you, and me, and all the rest.' Hand on his nape, Angelina turned him round. 'Don't worry about it baby. Your Granddad won't hurt none. And he had a good long life.'

'And is that where your Dad is?' Once when he'd asked, Angelina had said she had no Dad. But Uncle Gerard had told him how babies were made; had shown him the bull with his moaning wives. Babies came from a mother and a father, in violence and noise; even he knew that. 'Well, is he, Angelina?' If her Dad was there, at least Gramps would have company.

Angelina grinned showing her broken front tooth. 'Guess he will be,' she said. She turned away to survey the shifting mourners; squawked. 'If they don't hurry up, half these will join him. Lord Jesus, they'll get pneumonia.' The dog crept closer and Angelina gave it a quick kick. From long habit it skipped out of reach and stood wagging its ratty tail.

'Now Cris. You go back to the church and pay your Granddad your respects.'

Back in the church, he leant his head against his mother's dark coat, felt her arm curl round him and press him to her side, her fingers tickling the arch of his ribs. Just like a skinned rabbit, she'd say. The fingers slid up to his cold cheek.

A stirring at the front of the church. The priest had finished, the men were trooping forward and turning his eyes into her hand, he felt the tick, tick of his lashes on her palm.

'Don't look,' she whispered, and he tried to close his eyes, but somehow his lids popped open against the red glow between her gloved fingers, and like a jigsaw there came wood and brass, pieces of cloth over strong muscles rocking up and down; then suddenly, framed perfectly between her finger and thumb, he saw his father's face, gloomy and yearning, and he knew that it was truly Gramps inside the box.

A groaning of the heavy door, always stuck in winter, then a gust of cold air and his mother's hand dropped away and he looked up at milky clouds of incense and breath floating towards the shadowy roof, and then down the wall to Saint Cristòfol, his Christ-child heavy on his shoulders, the poor giant's expression puzzled, while the indifferent small fish nibbled on.

People started to move away from the front of the church; first Grandma titupping alone, almost a stranger in her black, smart coat. Through the veil, her face was familiar, eyes red, but there was something queer about the lips parted in an almost smile over teeth a little brown but all her own; how proud she was of them. She certainly wasn't the Grandma of yesterday who'd wept and wailed and begged all around her in the Chapel of Rest to tell what would become of her.

'And you,' she'd shrieked at Cris's mother, 'You think now you'll be queen.' And she'd looked across at Aunty Fina's small yellow face and then up at Uncle Gerard, and said in a whisper which was almost a shout. 'You shall do what you like with the house my darling.'

'Our house?' Cris had asked as he'd been bundled out. He'd tried not to breathe the air round that diminished, mushroom-coloured face so still on the yellow silk cushion in the open box, and now he sucked in air.

'Silly child,' his mother replied. 'The house is Grandma's, and when she dies, your father's.' And then she'd turned to his father following after.

'Are you going to let him pull the place down?' And when he'd replied quietly. 'He won't pull it down,' she'd shrieked, 'You fool. You'll let him do it. Fight a little for me, your children at least.'

His father had said softly. 'They aren't my enemies, Solange, they are my family.' To which she'd replied. 'They are my enemies,' and she'd turned back and Cris had turned too, and there was Gerard smiling in the doorway of the cold little room, his arms tight round Grandma and cousin Marta.

Watching his mother stare towards the door, Cris thought she had the same look now, angry and scared, while her hands stole up and down the front of her coat.

'Mama.' He tugged at one of those restless caressing hands. 'Come on. Everyone's going out.'

Mama didn't answer, but pulled down the veil from the brim of her hat and pushed him before her down the aisle and out through the narrow door where on the steep steps the snow lay in stained cushions.

Cris turned from giving Blanca cake and stared up through the straw-dust murk at this almost-stranger in dark suit and tie; but there was still something very Uncle Gerard about the way the tie was crooked and the wine-stain showed on the snowy shirt-front.

'Bit much? Funerals and all that?' He leant against the wood rail. 'You loved the old guy?'

He nodded. It was true, he'd loved Gramps. But Gramps seemed a long way away, and that wasn't really why he'd come down here. It was too hard to explain, except that there were a lot of people in the room only used for special occasions, all teeming in to kiss Grandma and then to take their glass of wine, their cake. But when Angelina had come to the door, Grandma had trotted forward with astonishing speed and spreading her arms had stood there, blocking the door.

'Fucking old cow,' Angelina had said as the door banged in her face.

'Your mama's taking it hard,' said Uncle Gerard.

Was that what made mama drink glass after glass of wine, until his father finally came and took the glass away from her, and she'd turned pink-nosed, pink-eyed, clutching at his arm, begging him to take care of her and her babe; an insult really to call him a babe. All the while one white hand stroked the flat front of her dress. Uncle Gerard stood there too, looking ... .   Well Cris wasn't sure how he'd been looking except it wasn't his usual Gerard look, as if life was a good joke.

It was then he'd gone down to the pigs, found Angelina, who'd kissed him, said nothing, and left.

'Fat enough now to kill, ain't they,' said Uncle Gerard.

'We can't do that Uncle Gerard. Grandma said!'

'Can't have a party. But the rest,' scratching a domed back.

Cris stared at his uncle. Mama wouldn't like it, he wanted to shriek, she doesn't like blood, and she's sad, and maybe she'll go back to France and I'll never see her again. But the words would not come out, and the pigs snuffled happily at his dangling fingers as he turned away from his uncle's red, smiling face.

'Please. We can't kill the pigs, Uncle Gerard. We're in mourning.'

SPRING

Gauging spate, balance,
depth, slippage – crossing mountain
torrents; fearful art.

Valerie Rymarenko

#4 FESTIVAL

Carnival or Carnestoltes.

There is no set date for this festival as it revolves around the date of the start of Lent, a movable fast that depends on the moveable feast of Easter.

This is typical as the first thing to realise is that there are no fixed rules about Carnival or Carnestoltes. Even the word Carnestoltes swirls with confusion. It can refer to Carnival itself or to King Carnestoltes who is a figure similar to Tudor England's Lord of Misrule. He in turn can be a stuffed effigy, sometimes resembling a leading political figure, and strung up high above the main town square to oversee the revelries. But equally he can be an actor or singer dressed up in crazy clothes and in charge of leading days of rowdy carousing .

As well as traditional parades and fancy dress balls, each year Andorra's comuns try to dream up something new. For example Encamp specialises in holding events at odd times: 4.05pm Trial of Smugglers followed by a sausage BBQ or 3.12am (sic) sweetmeats in the village hall. Carnestoltes (the actor) might open the festivities with a satirical speech singling out the key political events of the year, poking fun at government ministers or other important personages, never actually spelling out names but giving broad enough hints to keep the crowd chuckling. During the remaining days until Ash Wednesday he presides over masked balls, parades and all kinds of entertainments.

Finally in many parishes, on Shrove Tuesday, he, or the effigy, stands trial for bad behaviour and is sentenced to death. After reading his last will and testament – always permeated with the message to enjoy life to the full – the effigy is taken down and burned in the main square. (Happily the actor is more often 'buried'). The Carnival King has become scapegoat for all the mayhem of Carnival. There follows the seven weeks of austerity and abstinence which is Lent.

ACTRESS FOR A DAY

by Clare Allcard

"It's OK for you," I said ruefully as they shepherded us across La Massana's busy high street. "You don't live here."

My companion, a young, slightly implausible blonde, giggled with embarrassment. We both had our hair baled up in large, Day-Glo-pink rollers. I for the first time in about twenty years. But there you are, they say one must suffer for one's art.

I'd always fancied being in films and here was my big chance. You know the sort of thing: extra walks across room. In blinding flash Director realises she's perfect for female lead in horror movie opposite Boris Karloff – well, I have been dreaming this dream for some time now.

'Our' TV series, "*Entre el Torb i la Gestapo*" ("Between the Torb [a local sort of blizzard that whips up snow lying on the mountains] and the Gestapo"), is set in Andorra in the 1940s. At least I think it is. No one actually explained the plot. They don't. Not to extras.

A quick glance round the hotel and I knew why they'd chosen it. It must have been the only one left in Andorra untouched since World War II. Wooden stairs led up to a corridor whose walls were covered in thick, Regency-stripe flock paper and dotted with faded black and white photographs showing droves of sheep in remote mountain pastures. Something had bitten large chunks out of the floor tiles.

My companion, Margarida, looked round anxiously and whispered "I need a pee-pee I'm so nervous!"

As I wandered off down the gloomy corridor in search of the facilities, it occurred to me that I wasn't nervous at all. Was I too old or could it be that Margarida took the 'instant fame' myth seriously? I found the lavatory, an antique job with a cistern touching the ceiling and a bit of frayed string to pull.

Next, they herded us into one of the bedrooms; quite spacious compared with the loose boxes hotels stable their guests in nowadays. It was stacked with 1940s clothes. All dark. I must say I was most impressed by Wardrobe. They took one look at each of us, glanced at the rail, and then swooped unerringly on something that fitted. Mind you Casting had been firm. 'No fat extras. We only have clothes for slim ones.' I'd been a wee bit anxious myself on that score. How to tell my husband my road to fame had been blocked because I couldn't fit into any of the clothes? Shoes were no problem. They had a great sack full. Mine were so comfortable I thought of walking off in them: low-heeled, leather lace-ups with a soft, quilted lining.

Next, a pair of thick black tights was waved in my direction swiftly followed by a calf-length black and white flecked, genuine 1940s frock (later I found a genuine 1940s hole in it), then a black cardigan and a black coat with a fake-fur collar. A black handbag completed my ensemble.

Coat buttoned, I turned to weigh up the competition. Margarida looked smarter than me. Her dark brown outfit included rather handsome brown shoes and a little brown hat with netting dangling from it. They hadn't given me a hat. But of course she couldn't wear hers, not till they'd taken the rollers out. Then there was Elia. They dressed her up as a maid. She'd got a wicker carpet beater as a prop. Elia had huge, dark, smudgy eyes and a teasing smile. Still, poor dear, she couldn't be considered real competition, not dressed as a maid.

At the very last moment, as we were being bundled back downstairs, I remembered to grab my book and reading glasses. I might be a novice but I did know one thing: being an extra involves lots of waiting around.

Dressed in our 1940s finery, we trouped back across the high street and down to the Hair Trailer stationed at the bottom of the municipal car park. Ushered in, I made myself comfy and was just imagining my name in lights above the makeup mirror and wondering idly whether perhaps I should adopt a pseudonym, when I was ordered out again. A Star was approaching! Unfamiliar with Catalan television I don't know whether the bloke was a big star or a little one, but he made the most peculiar noises; as if he was practicing for the part of a Pyrenean bear. He kept growling. No one seemed to notice so I just looked the other way. After all if the chap felt better for a good growl, why not?

Outside, I paced up and down, glad of the coat and the thick tights. Nearby, another woman in rollers paced in the opposite direction. I noticed her stylish suit with envy. How come I hadn't got one like that? Then I saw her shoes. New. The real giveaway, though, were her stockings: sheer and with a very straight seam up the back. No thick peasant jobs for her. And no way did she find that outfit slung on a rail in the first floor bedroom. Despite an unpromising profile, not helped by her hair being in rollers, this too must be a Star.

Once the Bear was done, I was called back. Unfortunately Hair possessed a strong sense of hierarchy. If the Star was a Pyrenean bear then, she made it quite plain, I was a Pyrenean flea. She even removed my curlers with contempt. Then the Star of the seamed stockings appeared at the door. Back out in the cold for me; awfully good for inflated egos being an extra. Next time a much more friendly hairdresser called me in.

By the time she'd finished I looked just like photos of my mother during the war; a couple of tortoiseshell combs holding the hair tight at the temples and then bundles of curls frothing behind the ears. She tried sweeping my fringe up and back in a fashionable quiff; then took one look at my large, bony forehead and thought better of it. Hiding the forehead under another strategic cluster of curls, she grabbed a make-up tray and painted my lips vermillion. I was done.

Alone and incognito - there was no way any friend I met in the street would recognise me now - I drifted back to the hotel's dining room. This had been set aside for the cast. All of us. Very egalitarian. Here we extras received a pep talk from Sergi, a young lad in a baseball cap.

"*Never* look at the camera! Keep *absolutely* quiet during takes. When a take is over return to your original position. Finally, be careful of your clothes. They are valuable antiques." At least I think that is what he said. Trouble is, my Catalan's not that good. At the outset Sergi had asked me,

"Do you understand Catalan?"

I replied, "Provided you don't speak too fast."

He proceeded to mow me down with a Kalashnikov spray of words. Still he did have a sweet smile.

By now it was 7pm and our male counterparts had appeared. Margarida's brother, Pere, looked magnificent as a *contrabandista*: black beret perched rakishly above thick, black brows, crooked, hawk nose and piercing grey-blue eyes. A five-day growth of beard skulked ruffian-like round his jowls. Had he grown it specially? Another chap, very 1940s Dapper Gentleman, complained his hair felt as if it was glued down with honey. He was to be Margarida's husband and had to carry an empty suitcase.

Why oh why, do they insist on using empty suitcases? No one seems to know how to carry them as if they're full, and it's so irritating when they're wafted about like fly swats.

By now I was feeling a bit peckish and will say this for the acting life, there's a non-stop supply of food. Bags of croissants and pastries kept arriving along with bars of chocolate. Coffee and tea were on constant tap plus hot chocolate and fruit juice. Later, we were served an excellent, hot, à la carte dinner. For now I chose a croissant - and then spent anxious moments trying to brush the flakes out of my fake fur. I noticed the Stars only toyed with the occasional infusion. Probably worried about their figures, poor loves.

Elia had disappeared with Miguel who was playing the hotel's general dogsbody. Unfortunate man. Was it the excitement or were his hormones playing him up? Certainly, he had a wretched complexion. Elia had the carpet beater.

7.10pm time to get out my book. Will my reading glasses mark the bridge of my nose?

8.05pm The men start a game of cards.

10pm We all break for supper.

Back in the common room, I'm well dug into Alaska circa 1930, when Sergi returns. They're ready for my first take. I am to sit at a table in the bar and order a coffee from Miguel.

Alarmed, I ask, "Do I have to speak?"

I receive a pitying glance. "Of course not!"

Silly me. I wouldn't be an extra if I spoke.

The bar has been transformed. 1940s adverts hang behind the counter. A large wireless set squats on the floor. In the far corner, the Stars prepare themselves for shooting. Two pretty young women sit in large armchairs, their feet demurely crossed at the ankles. But oh dear, they are sitting far too far back. Surely everyone knows that in those days ladies never leant back in their chairs; it was considered slouching.

The camera is on rails. Pere is at the bar holding a glass of something red and vile, presumably imitation wine. Sergi places me at a table by the door from where I have an excellent view of the proceedings.

Then, the Assistant Director himself comes over! My moment has come. I give him my most dazzling smile. That does it! For a split second he looks at me – then taps the chair opposite and tells me to change places. He prefers that I sit with my back to the camera.

Never mind. No doubt one can ooze character just as successfully through a well-focused back. I contemplate my role; a lone woman of a certain age gracing an Andorran café during the war. Not two feet behind me sits a smuggler. I will clutch my handbag to my bosom and sit very, very upright.

The Assistant Director comes over again. He smiles. My heart leaps.

"Put your handbag on the table there."

"Do you think I should," I ask doubtfully. Misguided young man. He clearly knows nothing about history. Does he really imagine a lone woman would have exposed her handbag on the table? In those days? Besides it looks untidy.

Sergi now approaches with a Spanish copy of Life Magazine circa 1954. He searches through it till he comes to a page with an advertisement for sewing machines. "There," he says, "You can read that page," and smiles his puckish smile.

"I hate to tell you, but in the 40s it was considered very *mal educat* to read at table." He looks at me as if I am quite mad then moves off. Someone brings me a cup and saucer, a china jug and a sugar bowl with no sugar in it. They've put a teabag in the cup, the nasty paper bit dangling outside.

The Assistant Director comes back to tell someone to put sugar in the bowl.

"*Perdoni*," I say. "I'm sure they didn't have teabags in Andorra in the 1940s." I proceed to stuff the little tag and string as well as the bag into the bottom of the cup. Maybe I can get a job in Continuity or Research. Though, by the looks of it, the budget for research has already run out. Suddenly, I'm startled by a roar stage left. My head whips round and I stare straight into the affronted gaze of The Bear. Clearly his idiosyncrasies are not supposed to be queried by mere extras.

Behind me tension mounts. A man appears at the door with one of those clapper boards. I'm furious. So much going on and I can't see a thing. Not to worry, I'm sitting very straight and will pour my tea with great character. Maybe later on some other film director, a more sensitive, perspicacious director, watching the finished production, will spot that hidden talent.

"Silence!"

"Roll!"

"Action!"

I pick up my jug and gracefully dribble a little water into the cup. Behind me the saloon doors swing open and a chap carrying a rucksack and snowshoes barges in. I can't see his face but he has a gorgeous voice.

For some unknown reason The Bear greets him in heavily accented English, then switches to Catalan and then again in English calls to Miguel, "Champagne! The best!"

Then we cut. We did that take six times, occasionally getting as far as the two female Stars also speaking in heavily accented English. Why, I hadn't a clue but I was dying to offer some elocution lessons.

The shooting of my scene being over, we extras were sent back to the sitting room. Elia had disappeared and Margarida was still waiting to do her bit. Then Sergi told us we could go home. It was almost midnight. We had to return our costumes to wardrobe, our hair combs to Hair and then collect our pay.

Margarida and I went upstairs; to find Elia the maid, totally transformed. She was now wearing a rather dashing, low cut dress, a jet necklace and new shoes! It was those smouldering eyes that did it. She'd been spotted by the director. Her next part was as a coquette chatting up the barman.

Some people have all the luck.

So, to the big question. Will I actually be on television? Well, probably not if Pere, the *contrabandista*, is to be believed. From where he sat he could see the film monitor. As the man pushed through the saloon doors and the camera slid silently towards us, there was a split second when you could just see half of Pere's face. For less than a split second you could also see a few locks of my hair. Ah well, at least they paid me thirty pounds and I got to be an actress for a day.

* * * * * * * * * *

Andorra's Freedom Trails.

Later I was to discover that "Between the Torb and the Gestapo" was in fact a four part, Catalan TV3 series based on Francesc Viadiu Vendrell's autobiography of the same name. Viadiu tells of the Second World War collaboration between members of the Catalan and Occitan/French resistance. How they organised an escape route or Freedom Trail, from Toulouse through the mountains of Andorra to Barcelona ensuring the survival, among others, of a group of downed British airmen being pursued by the Gestapo, and carrying crucial information intended for British Intelligence. Hotel Palanques, where my part of the series was shot, was the safe house where many escapees stayed. Today it has been completely renovated and, in the little square opposite are two memorials (one erected by the British Embassy, the other by the Andorran Government), listing the brave members of the resistance who risked their lives in the Allied cause: Joaquim Baldrich Forné, Salvador Calvet Pal, Antoni Fornè Jou, Eduard Francesc and Lluís Molné Armengol, Josep Monpel Querol and Albert Vicente Conejos.

AN HONOURABLE PROFESSION

A picture of the smuggling trade in Andorra

by J. P. Wood

I started my career in smuggling quite young. Sweet seventeen and returning from Germany to my school in Oxford, I used to smuggle the odd bottle of duty-free gin from the NAAFI for my father's UK stockpile. Do you remember that time of meanness when the limit was a half-bottle of spirits? Well my Dad had the lovely belief that if he poured out an inch or so to make a pink gin, no self-respecting customs' man would consider the bottle anything else but half-full. Wrong. My best friend and I took revenge on the swingeing duty I had to pay by consuming the remains of the bottle with some rather greasy fish and chips. No tonic though, we were too broke.

I determined that was the end of my smuggling career. The very thought of it brought me out in a cold sweat, possibly the ghost of that early ginny hangover. Ah well, the best laid plans...

If I were male, young, and Andorran, it would be very different. I should simply be following in the footsteps of my father, grandfather and probably great, great, great-grandfather in an honourable profession.

Andorra was destined to be a smugglers' paradise. From 1468 onwards, it gained extraordinary tax advantages, including the right to hold a tax-exempt fair every two weeks, plus exemption from taxes on products brought in from outside the Principality. Add to that a labyrinth of steep mountain tracks leading out of the country, secret except to the gentlemen of the road. Stir into the mixture the independent spirit of the average Andorran and acute poverty which meant that any family here had to make what money they could. Bordering Andorra were Spain and France, imposing harsh taxes on a range of goods: it was smuggling in the making

The main contraband of Andorra is tobacco. The cultivation of tobacco in the country began in the 17th century, half a century after the plant was introduced to Europe from the Americas. Tobacco was made a royal monopoly in France and Spain, and in Spain the death penalty was imposed on the illegal cultivation and sale of the plant.

It is written that:

In 1733, the two states demanded that the Episcopal Co-Prince, the Bishop of Urgell, put an end to this maleficent contraband. Bending in the wind to superior forces, he sent out a decree commanding the Andorrans to destroy their crops and to stop all further tobacco cultivation. Over 200 armed Andorrans opposed the men sent by the Bishop to tear up their harvest. But, in 1735 the decree was implemented and some of the men jailed and some deported.

I don't suppose this stopped the cultivation in Andorra of tobacco but it somewhat dampened the trade for the next hundred or so years.

Smuggling boomed again in the nineteenth century. Like most impoverished people, the Andorrans learnt to seize the moment and tobacco was not the only item smuggled.

One source asserts that at the end of the nineteenth century when France declared a monopoly on that household essential, the sulphur match, the Andorrans set up a factory for their production. All that was necessary to import was sulphur since pine, the wood of choice, grew in abundance. And then hey-ho, hey-ho, on with the rucksacks, square packs covered in sacking which could carry up to 30 kg, and over the passes with a commodity infinitely lighter than tobacco, although that trade continued. I have not found confirmation of this, but I like to think that it is an example of the independent and creative Andorran spirit.

There are other more verifiable incidents. Franco banned the import of mules to Spain as they were being sold to the Republicans. Andorrans smuggled them in from France, pastured them in the mountains during the summer then moved them across the southern border.

An article in the weekly magazine devoted to popular music, *Billboard*, on 29th August, 1960, recounted that the presence of banned US Juke Boxes in France was due to their being smuggled by sea to Barcelona and then taken to Andorra by truck. Andorra was not obliged to pay duty on these. It was only a short step to take the coin machines into France where many a village café enjoyed the proceeds. 1961 saw the end of this profitable little number in the freight-forwarding business (smuggling) when the French decided to abolish duty on them.

Other items smuggled through the last centuries included olive oil, petrol, silk stockings, perfumes, make-up, cars and lace. A friend of mine told me that the latter was taken across the border wound around the hairy torsos of the smugglers. Imagine on warm days, delicate lace-adorned women feeling an unexpected frisson provoked by the fugitive whiff of masculine sweat and tobacco.

Perhaps one of the strangest tales I heard was told by a friend whose family have lived in Arinsal and run a business there forever and a day. 'I went ghost hunting,' said Josep. 'I was twenty-one.' Well he is fifty-four now so you may figure out the year. His best friend in mischief phoned him quite late one summer night. 'Josep,' he said, 'you've got to come. I've seen a ghost on Coll de la Botella.' (Skiers will know that this is up past the ski station to Pal and, except in winter, from there you can take a rough track to Spain). So off Josep went and met his friend at the junction. Like two naughty schoolboys, they crept along the dark road, were startled by a car roaring out of a wooden barn - smugglers or illicit lovers they never knew. 'There,' breathed his friend. They gazed entranced at pale, small moons dancing over the slopes, graceful but inexplicable. For a while the young men watched, puzzled and a little scared; then chilled they made their ways home.

A few days later, Josep and his friend were disappointed to read in the newspapers that their phantom dancers were the work of a middle-aged Dutchman trapping moths on the mountainside for export and sale abroad - even then this was illegal, and he was arrested and I suppose paid a large fine. The pale, dancing moons had been the lights he used to lure the insects into his net.

Smuggling out the corpses of poor insects! Whatever next?

The commerce in cars has occasioned more sinister events: like the time there was car smuggling from Spain to behind the Iron curtain and someone cheated on the gang. His body was found in a burnt out 4x4 on the Coll d'Ordino. The murderers were caught after a citizen of Encamp reported seeing a foreign car driving through town at 3am in the morning.

As in all countries, smuggling has been and is for profit. The profession became truly worthy of being termed 'honourable' during the Carlist, Francoist and two World Wars. Escapees from these horrors were smuggled through this tiny country by people of great courage either towards France to escape from the clutches of Spain, or in the case of marooned allied airman, soldiers and fugitive Jews, towards neutral Portugal.

Smuggling has not always been one way. During the Second World War, wool was in short supply and for three years it was smuggled into Andorra from the Pallars (part of Catalonia). The shepherds and smugglers of the region certainly earned their considerable profits; the way to Andorra was through steep and difficult terrain well-guarded by bands of Spanish Guardia Civil, and there was always the chance of an even more dangerous clash with their own kind.

Clashes of this type are not unknown. In January 1993, I was dining with some friends whose *xalet* was the last on the then un-metalled track leading to La Rabassa, a wide plateau with easy access into Spain. (It became less accessible during the late nineties when Spain cracked down on tobacco smuggling. Patrols of Guardia Civil frequently blocked the jeep tracks with coiled barbed wire and raised weapons.) At this time though, it was quiet enough, until the small hours of the morning when we and other guests were taking coffee and thinking of home. A cacophony of sirens and a dazzle of lights brought us all to the front of the house to be startled by ambulances and police cars charging past.

In the newspapers the next day, we read that two gangs of tobacco smugglers had clashed and that one member had been shot in the cheek, not by the police, we were assured. Arrests had been made.

There are of course rumours of 'other-way' smuggling. Young Andorran friends of mine have told me that you can find illegal substances on offer in the discotheques. Before you go in search of the 'candy' of your choice, do bear in mind that the Police here are protective of their young people, and effective. The trade is limited compared to most countries and the charming trader you approach may well be a plain-clothes policeman. The penalties and sentencing are severe. So stick to wine and whisky, legal and inexpensive, but treat alcohol with the respect granted to it by most Andorrans. Drunken driving is treated harshly too.

There is one family that I know of whose great uncle was shot dead by the Guardia Civil during Franco's time, but generally smuggling has been a reasonably friendly affair, with frontier guards withholding fire if the smugglers dropped their goods and moved away.

In 1996-7 things began to change. Investigations into tobacco smuggling in Spain, Britain and France seemed to indicate that every Andorran national, man, woman and child, was smoking sixty-eight cigarettes a day. The European union came to the conclusion that in that year alone, they had lost some 400 million Euros in tax revenue. Small wonder that the Andorran government on the 10th of

June 1999 was *persuaded* to take measures declaring the honourable profession a crime.

Criminalisation of smuggling certainly has not brought the occupation to an end. In 2013, the Guardia Civil seized more than 10,600 cartons of cigarettes, along with 325 kilograms of rolling tobacco, altogether worth around €500,000.

Money smuggling is not quite on a par with tobacco smuggling but over recent months it has become a more serious issue. The disclosure, last year, that Jordi Pujol, ex-President of Catalonia, had salted away large sums in Andorra, plus other economic factors, has driven many Spaniards to withdraw their funds from the country's banks. There is a limit of €10,000 on cash taken out of the country without being declared by the bearer. The Frontier Police and their specially trained sniffer dogs are on the lookout for anything suspicious. Not so long ago, an elderly couple tried to smuggle out their life-savings and were caught; we suspect someone ratted. They lost everything except the statutory undeclared €10,000, and probably most of that disappeared in the fine.

Others are more canny and the newspaper, *El País*, speaks of a man with money in Andorra, who travelled into the country with three friends. There was about €100,000 in the account, and he withdrew €36,000. The four travellers returned to Spain with €9,000 each, a little under the legal limit. They repeated this until the account was emptied.

No official figures are available yet for 2014, but in 2013 the Guardia Civil seized some €3.1 million in cash, almost three times the amount confiscated in 2012.

Local, regional and national newspapers give reports of huge hauls of cigarettes and other tobacco products by customs officers, and accounts of arrests of numbers of people, some from Andorra, many from Catalonia, and some from as far afield as Malaga and the *País Basc* including left wing politicians, ex-mayors and many ordinary chancers. In all the newspapers you will find photos of pyramids of cigarettes and other tobacco products, accounts of massive fines and sharp prison sentences. Still the trade continues.

And so too do the tales.

At the beginning of this article I declared that I could never smuggle, but I did, inadvertently, a long time ago before the "Old King" Franco died, or rather before the young King Juan Carlos came to Spain's throne. I worked briefly in Andorra with a school friend as a *Fixer* translating for the Anglophone community, making industrial quantities of Christmas cakes, or ferrying people and objects. We were asked by someone from the ex-pat community to fetch a parcel from an office in Barcelona.

A day in the great city, and we would get paid!

As we went through customs towards Spain, we were stopped and our transport, a Mini-Moke, hideously uncomfortable, but much loved, was taken apart. There we were, two young and pretty useless females in the middle of the customs' zone, trying ineptly to screw the sides back on a car principally held together by rust. Fortunately some kindly Australians gave us a hand, and off we set.

Even more fortunately, on the way back, we were not stopped. How fortunate we had been, we didn't know, until a friend told us that we had brought back a hefty portion of pornography. From Franco's Spain? Into Andorra where at the time such things were a definite 'no-no'?

That was one client less.

My sister, who has lived here for forty-five years, has a rather more sinister smugglers' tale, also from the very early seventies.

In the centre of Andorra La Vella, there was an inn, *El Faisa*, or the Pheasant as it was known to its habitués. It is now quite a chic restaurant; then it was a little shabby, a little louche, meeting place for Anglophones, and also a cheap place to stay the night. The jolly hostess was enchanted when three good-looking young Dutch fellows booked rooms for three months while they 'looked around at business opportunities'. They were charming, generous, a particularly attractive trait to the young entrepreneurs who were frequently near the breadline.

Oh the shock when suddenly the boys were no longer to be seen in Claudia's jolly bar! Bills were not paid, and their Mustang sat forlorn on the pavement of the narrow street outside. Then, one evening, someone came into the bar brandishing a Spanish newspaper bearing on the front page a photo of the three boys looking not quite so dashing as they were carted away by the Dutch police.

It turned out that not only had they been dealing in drugs, but that the body parts of one of their young female mules (human) had been found scattered along the perimeter of the new motorway outside Barcelona.

Smuggling is big business nowadays, more likely to use a pantechnicon than human mules. However, traditions die hard.

So should you be walking in the mountains near either of the two frontiers, and should you meet some battered looking jeeps driven by sturdy men with weather-beaten faces and not a single designer sports garment between them, my advice to you is to give them a cheery *'Bon Dia'* and to continue on your way.

An eccentric young lady from Erts
Once rented a lorry from Hertz
She travelled Andorra
In chemise and fedora
And quite gave up the wearing of skirts

SPORTING ANDORRA

by Iain Woolward

Shortly after being asked to write a piece about sport in Andorra, I came across a news report on Reuters' web site: half a million golfers around the planet had recently given up the game; they simply no longer had the spare four and a half hours it takes to slog around eighteen-hole golf courses. Right next to that piece was one about how the total, global audience for televised sports events was continuing to break records, pushing the values of major sports franchises to unheard-of heights: $3.44 billion for Real Madrid, for example. The conclusion was clear: participating in a sport can be time consuming and jolly tiring; better to simply watch other people have a go. Sports stadia have become the cathedrals of our time; so essential to our communities that local municipalities erect them at the tax payers' expense in the hope that the billionaire franchise owners will deem them fit for purpose.

There's a further disincentive to actually *doing* a sport: the avalanche of TV advertising cash flowing to athletes – performers – enables them not only to quit their day jobs but also to spend every waking hour attaining mesmerizing levels of excellence at things that used to be considered just a bit of fun, usually involving balls of some kind. The gap between what we used to think was attainable and what we see can actually be attained has become an unbridgeable chasm of gloom. Goals are important in all sports, not just soccer. If you know there's no way in hell that you'll be any good at something, why bother with it? If you personally have no more chance of, for example, hitting a golf ball three and a half times the length of a football pitch (the current *average* for a professional golfer) than clean-jerking 263.5 kilos/581 lbs (the current world record), it's a lot easier on the ego to simply gawk at somebody else doing so.

But what has any of this got to do with Andorra? It's this: in Andorra this whole shift from active to passive is set in reverse. Even by micro-country standards (Andorra has the same population as, for example, Barrow-in-Furness in England and Matanuska-Susitna in Alaska), the facilities here for watching other people play some sport or other are skimpy, at best. The national sports stadium has 1,299 seats - about a fifth the capacity of Barrow-in-Furness' soccer club. And only occasionally do they have bums on all of them. On the other hand the country is stuffed with facilities for actually *doing* a bewildering array of athletic activities, both summer and winter.

Before launching into the menu of the country's sporting possibilities, I should 'fess up. Andorrans *do* get very excited about watching F.C. Barcelona – the finest soccer club in the world (at least according to Andorrans). However this needs to be judged in a political, rather than sporting context. When iron-fisted Franco ruled neighbouring Spain, associating oneself with the culture of independently-inclined north-eastern Spain – Catalonia - was illegal. Speaking Catalan got people shot. Turning up to a football match didn't. Supporting the region's premier club, 'Barça', became a relatively safe expression of the independent Catalonian spirit, especially when Franco's home team, Real Madrid, came to town. The region's separatist hankerings are as strong as ever and, as I write, are still thwarted by Madrid. Supporting FC Barcelona remains a collective expression of Catalonian spirit; Andorra's successful defence of its own sovereignty naturally brings it into alignment with its Catalonian cousins.

Andorra has two rugby clubs and two football clubs – one of which, many years ago, actually eliminated F.C. Barcelona en route to winning the regionally important Catalonian Cup. The country always puts up a national team for tennis' Davis Cup; is always represented at both the winter and summer Olympics; it constantly hosts world championships for various summer and winter sports that require mountains; it offers two world-class mountain bike parks and, come winter, 200 miles/320 kilometers of copiously groomed 'piste'.

Over 80% of Andorra is open land, about 150 square miles/387 square kilometres of magnificent mountain-hiking terrain, networked by over 50 properly-maintained trails (should you wish to use one). This tiny country boasts multiple adventure parks, three golf courses (of varying lengths), and more publically-accessible sports centres per head of population than any other country in the world. I could go on and on, but you get the idea. People *DO* sports here. In fact, they DO a lot of stuff. Take singing: currently there are twelve choirs belting it out in Andorra, all with an eye to the annual Aplec (gathering) at which they will perform independently and then combine into one massive choir of four hundred souls, ringing out as one. In terms of percentage participation by country's native adults that's the equivalent of about seven million Americans belting out the 'Star Spangled Banner'. Most Andorran choirs are subsidized by their local town council ('*Comú*') so, while performances are not judged nor prizes awarded, a competitive spirit lingers on from when, only three generations ago, rivalries flourished between isolated villages separated as they were by hours of slogging over mountain tracks.

A tiny country with a maximum income tax rate of 10% doesn't have a ton of dosh to throw at the vanity-inspired business of winning Olympic medals – especially after it's paid for a slew of excellent facilities, indoors and out, for its citizenry at large. Publicly funded support for individual sportsmen and women is, well...non-existent. And since Olympians are unique in the televised sports world in that they are not paid directly to compete, it's tough to medal at the Olympics on your own dime. No Andorran ever has. Their world-class results pop up in less-professionalized sports like 'Pitch and Putt Golf' (World Championship Silver Medal, 2006; Bronze, 2008) and 'Ski Mountaineering' (World Championship Bronze Medal, 2009). Even though the country is a skiing Mecca, Andorran skiers with Olympic aspirations have to tag along with other countries' teams to get a decent training. That will only take you so far - usually mid-double figures - when it comes to Olympic or World Cup skiing.

But if you talk to Andorrans about national sports you don't get the down-at-mouth moaning that typifies, for example, English soccer fans, droning on as they do about the latest denial of what should rightfully be theirs: global conquest. Instead, your eyes will mist up as you are regaled with one story or another of individual struggle. For example: there's a guy in Andorra who has won the Paris-Dakar Rally (driver; rally car division) twice, but is arguably less cherished here than an Andorran rally driver who hasn't won even *one* Dakar Rally - or any other rally for that matter. His name is Albert Llovera.

When Albert was seventeen years old he competed in the giant slalom in the 1984 Winter Olympics – the youngest guy there and still the second youngest winter Olympian ever. He came 48th out of 60; OK for a rookie. At the next year's European Championships he was thundering down the giant slalom when a rather confused Swiss judge wandered across the course. Albert hit him doing over 70mph/112kph. The impact shattered Albert's sternum, snapped half his ribs clean in two and severed his spinal cord just below the shoulders. He'd never walk again, let alone ski. (The Swiss guy got away with a broken hip).

It took a while, but one day, after months of intensive and depressing rehab, Albert figured out that spending the rest of his life - or even the rest of that insightful day - in a rage born of a fruitless pursuit of physical restoration was a waste of his time. His mother, however, continued to be really pissed off about the situation and literally dragged her son around to every physiotherapist, acupuncturist and plain old-fashioned quack within a day's drive of Andorra - anyone who could offer any hope that her son might not have to spend the rest of his life in a wheelchair. She was – and is - a great mum, but a lousy driver. To the mental battering Albert was going through from the accident was now being added the anguish of enduring his mum's chronic inadequacies at the wheel.

After weeks – months - of being shouted and cussed at, his mum yelled back (in Catalan), 'OK, wise guy, from now on *you* do the driving!'

They fixed up the family saloon with entirely-manual controls. Things looked up; courtesy of his in-born urge to excel and the challenges of the winding Pyrenean mountain roads, Albert turned into a hell of a driver. One winters' evening, after what had already been a long day on the road, he wheeled himself back out to the car, dragged himself into the driver' seat, eased off the handbrake and rolled silently into the darkness. Some buddies had said they'd be getting together that night to race their souped-up 4x4's around a course of hay bales set up in a snow-covered and otherwise empty car park at one of the ski resorts. When Albert arrived they assumed it was to watch. But after a couple of runs he was whipping the family saloon around those bales faster than any of his buddies. His legs were shot, but he still had the reaction time of an Olympic downhill skier. Folks took notice, including the local Fiat rep. The factory teamed him up with a co-driver/navigator of repute, Diego Vallejo, and put him on the Junior World Rally circuit. Success there led to a place on the Super 2000 World Rally circuit in which Albert finished 5th in class on his first outing. As I write, he's still at it. Getting better all the time.

And so: if all you want to do is live vicariously in the glow of accomplishments of individuals, clubs and countries competing and winning on the world stage, Andorra is probably not for you. But if you enjoy getting out and chasing your own athletic demons, the freedom and opportunity to do so in Andorra is tough to beat. And, if the statistics are to be believed, sucking that thin mountain air into your lungs could add a dozen years to your active life.

A denizen of fair La Massana
Had her eyes firmly fixed on Nirvana.
Well she got there all right
When she swiftly took flight
On the skin of a rotten banana

#5 FESTIVAL

by Clare Allcard

SANT JORDI: THE DAY OF THE BOOK AND THE ROSE

8.30am! Help! Late as usual. I should be half way down the mountain by now. For this is the 23rd April, St George's Day (Sant Jordi to Catalans) and our Andorra Writers' Group has reserved a stand in the Plaça del Poble, the capital's main square. Tradition dictates that today all the females of Andorra and Catalonia, from little girls to old ladies, present a book to their favourite males: be they lover, teacher, father or grandson. It is also the day when all the males of the species are expected to present the females closest to their hearts with a single, wine-red rose.

The Day of the Book and the Rose indeed! Surely the world's most civilised festival with its symbols of wisdom, culture and love.

Sant Jordi is the day when the bookshops – and the authors - of the region expect to make a killing. As I write, throughout Catalonia they are hoping to sell a whopping 800,000 books, half their annual turnover, in just one or two days. Not so long ago, when Andorra's total population stood at 65,000, Andorran males bought 70,000 red roses. Tradition writ large!

My diminutive 4x4 van is already stacked high with fruit-crates of second-hand books and, naturally, in this polyglot country, they come in a choice of four languages: Catalan,

Spanish, French and English. They are to be sold at 1€ each for the local charity, "Infants del Món". There is also one box, more gently nurtured, full of new volumes of the books we have written ourselves.

But from whence comes this remarkable custom? In centuries past, St George was one of Christendom's most popular patron saints, and even today he not only keeps watch over Catalonia but England, Ethiopia, Georgia, Portugal, Russia, Ukraine, and a dozen countries more …. It was he who, born in Palestine, rode to the defence of a city – some say in the Middle East - besieged by a man-eating Dragon. Each day the citizens drew lots to see who next would be fed to the beast. Finally the lot fell to the king's own daughter. The beautiful princess had already been chained to a rock, waiting to be devoured, when St George rode to the rescue astride a white charger - naturally. George promised the citizens that, if they would only convert to Christianity, he would slay the Dragon and rescue the princess. According to legend, they did – and he did.

As with all good legends, that of Saint George and the Dragon has many versions. Catalans, for instance, may tell you that he didn't slay the Dragon in Arabia at all but right here in the heart of Catalonia; in the town of Montblanc to be precise, just a couple of hours drive from Andorra's southern border. Every year, on 23rd April, the people of Montblanc re-enact the story of Sant Jordi. They parade atop the walled town's wide ramparts bedecked in period costume. The procession ends at St George's Gate where there is a tiled plaque set in the thick stone walls announcing that this was the very spot where St George slew the Dragon and where the Dragon's blood gushed into the earth from whence a bush of red roses bloomed. So you see, it must be true!

As far back as 1463, Catalonia celebrated Sant Jordi as the Day of the Rose, the day of lovers, a Catalan St Valentine's. On the same day in the 19th century members of the Catalan parliament in Barcelona would honour the women who worked for them with red roses.

The van and I hurtle ever downwards, skimming through the lower gears as we approach the hairpins, speeding up on the straights, the crates in the back swishing back and forth as we go.

Arriving at the Plaça del Poble - in fact the roof of the government administration building - we weave cautiously across the square not wanting to add stall-holders' blood to that once spilled by the infamous Dragon. Stopping beside our stand, I begin to unload: cloths to cover the rough tables on loan from the local council, an essential Andorran blue, gold and red tricolour to pin to the stall front, signs in Catalan and English, price tags, sellotape. Add to that, thick blankets against the cold, swathes of plastic sheeting against possible rain, thermoses of hot coffee, plastic carrier bags full of – well, more plastic carrier bags, bum bags with spare change and, of course, books. Oh, and finally, packets of particularly scrumptious chocolate biscuits as morale-boosting comfort food.

For Sant Jordi, coming early in the year, can be a challenge even to the most hardy soul. It is quite common for an icy wind, straight off the capital's encircling white peaks, to chase across the square unsettling the books, colliding with buckets of roses and freezing the sellers to the bone. Of course there have been blessed occasions when the sun has blazed down to curl up the edges of the paperbacks, wilt the roses and send sellers searching for their sunscreen.

Already holders of some two dozen stands are in the process of rapid transformation, for all has to be in place to greet the capital's Mayor and her entourage of ministers and TV cameramen, by 10am.

So where did the idea of the books come from and what was the connection with Sant Jordi? In 1923, the Catalan parliament decided to include books in the ceremony of the rose. Why the 23rd of April? Because the 23rd April was the day, in 1616, that the great Spanish writer, Miguel de Cervantes, father of the European novel and author of *Don Quixote*, and the great English playwright, William Shakespeare, both died. At least that's the idea. Dig a little deeper and you will discover that in fact it was the day Cervantes was buried. He died on the 22nd. Dig deeper still and you will unearth the fact that, as the Spanish were already using the Gregorian Calendar and the English the ancient Julian one, Cervantes actually died 11 days before Shakespeare, who not only died but was also born on the 23rd April – Julian Calendar.

Now other members of our writers group appear and we rush to be ready for inspection. Beside us, sixth formers from the country's secondary schools turn up with buckets full of red roses, each bloom accompanied by a piece of wheat for fertility and all carefully wrapped in clear plastic and tied with a patriotic blue, gold and red ribbon. At 4€ a bloom, their roses do not come cheap but all the profit goes towards the class's summer outing.

Next, the crocodile processions arrive. Minute infants out of kindergarten, identified by florescent tabards emblazoned with their school's name, are kept together by a long rope from which gaily coloured cotton loops dangle down on either side. Each child has one tiny wrist held in a loop and the other hand free. With a teacher at the front to lead and at the back to scoop up any that might break free, they make an adorable and encouraging sight on their very first cultural outing. As they meander wide-eyed past the stalls they occasionally reach up to touch a book or gaze with longing at the velvety roses decorating our stall. Clearly Andorran educators have taken the dictum, "Give me a child until he is seven and I will give you the man." to heart.

Throughout the day "UNESCO Andorra" organises cultural events: maybe they have invited the parish's Giants, Charlemagne and Ermessenda, to dance. Made of papier mâché, King Charlemagne is 3.5 metres tall and weighs 50 kilos. Getting him to dance and pirouette requires considerable strength and skill. Or maybe members of the passing public are invited to come to the microphone to read a page or two from one of the books being launched that day until, by the end of the afternoon, a whole work has been read aloud.

The public arrives in waves: 10am, lunchtime and then a final surge between 6 and 8pm. Passing eyes shy nervously away from our English titles then settle with relief on boxes of children's books in French, Spanish and the country's official language, Catalan. Younger adults rifle through the mound of English paperbacks hoping to find some 'beach fiction' to improve their language skills.

By the time evening arrives we are wilting and ready to head home. We pile crates of books, now reduced in number, back into the van, carry our takings from the sale of second-hand books over to the "Infants del Món's" stall, put away the publicity and fold up the Andorran flag; all ready for the 23rd April next year.

Even as the planet gets warmer
The skiing'll be good in Andorra
As late as, say, Easter
They make snow on the piste
Confusing the poor local flora

SKULLDUGGERY IN ARINSAL

FICTION

by Iain Woolward

Nigel had come to Andorra to die, quietly. Of what, he knew yet not. Trampled to death by the march of time? Plain old heart failure? Perhaps killed off by some super-bug lingering up his nose (as super-bugs like to do), just itching to exploit signs of failing health? Regardless, what better spot in which to bump into one's Maker than this tiny, tidy country high in the Pyrenees? Clean air; magnificent scenery; friendly populace; all relatively affordable…handy should life linger longer than expected. Plus there exists in Andorra a fair smattering of readily available, well-travelled, multi-lingual acquaintances with whom to pass whatever time remains of their life's journey, or his, whichever turned out to be the shorter.

Andorra also enjoys one of the lowest crime rates of the developed world. According to Interpol, its incidences of assaults and robberies are on a par with Japan's, and remain so with considerably less policing.

As will become clear later, this story makes more sense if the reader understands that, by and large, Andorra's criminal mini-minority can be divided into three groups:

1. Those driven by passion, fuelled by alcohol, to over-react to a perceived slight. The 'perp' typically bashes away at some counter-party until such time as said slight is resolved. Only very rarely indeed does this end in death. Sometimes new friendships result.

2. Those who burn off whatever irks them by driving their cars at such orders of magnitude in excess of Andorra's liberal, largely unenforced speed limits that they may be considered 'criminals' rather than just ill-behaved. Typically the laws of physics bring the proceedings to a gory end, often memorialized by plastic flowers tied to dented crash barriers, or strewn here and there by the wind, their gaudy colours fast fading under the intense sunlight of these altitudes.

3. Those who come up to Andorra with only thieving in mind, attracted by hundreds of shop windows glittering with easily-fenced luxury goods. These individuals exhibit almost complete lack of foresight - some might say 'intelligence'. How else can one explain that, in casing the joint, they invariably fail to heed the fact that Andorra has but two driveable exits - one to Spain, the other France – both staffed by gaggles of gruff-looking customs agents, hell-bent on preventing their fellow countrymen from hauling more than the permitted allotment of duty-free goods back home from duty-free shopping sprees in Andorra. There are exceptions: recently two Rumanians were at least smart enough to figure out that, having nicked 6,000,000 euros-worth of jewellery, they should abandon their van and set out across the mountains to Spain on foot. Figuring they might be pursued by sniffer dogs, they obliterated their scent trails with liquid bleach, the eye-watering odour of which could be detected from hundreds of meters away by mere humans.

If you're wondering why 'smugglers' are not listed above as a 'criminal minority', the answer is this: smuggling is not considered much of a crime in Andorra. In fact not long ago it was a national sport; a right of manhood. Grim-faced men with huge thighs and barrel chests often hauled their own weight in contraband – mostly home grown tobacco – over the mountain passes at night. Try strolling over these old smuggling routes, even in broad daylight carrying only a sandwich and a couple of beers and you'll see why, during the current affluent period in Andorra's history, the locals have either gone off smuggling altogether or rely on false-bottomed trucks. Nevertheless there's still a lot more smuggling going on than is indicated by the much-publicized but relatively occasional arrests in Spain and France: the disparity between cigarettes imported directly into Andorra (upon which a mere 4.5% tax is levied) and the volume that could conceivably leave with duty-free splurging tourists suggests that every man, woman and child in Andorra is smoking six packs a day.

And so back to our tale of Nigel, the Andorran 'newby': it was eleven o'clock on a midweek night in November. After what he would call 'a mild libation' (eight large Glenlivets) knocked back at his primary watering hole in Arinsal (the Andorran ski-resort most favoured by the British), Nigel was ricocheting from wall to wall down a steeply inclined and ominously icy back ally. Suspecting that, should he end up horizontal, he'd lack the wherewithal to re-erect himself, he found comfort in the rough stonework that defined his route.

Perhaps that's why he was 'marked' by two 'perps' looking him over as he passed the doorway in which they lurked.

They'd left Perpignan early that morning, wound their way over the snowy pass into Andorra and packed the false floor and side-panels of their van with thousands of duty free cigarettes purchased over the course of the day in small lots from over a hundred duty-free shops. Having become overly excited about the easy 20% profit they'd make on each pack they sold upon their return to France, they'd spent just about every euro they had. The van now being almost out of fuel, this fiscal void had to be filled, pronto.

"Garble, garble, garble, immediatement!" was all Nigel heard when confronted by two hooded youths.

"I'm sorry……do you speak English?" Like the majority of his countrymen, Nigel had respectfully declined to learn Catalan – after all, he expected his time in Andorra to be short lived. He was also devoid of French – widely spoken in Andorra – due to the competing calls upon his attentions during French lessons at school, from whence he'd gone straight into the British army.

The question came as no surprise to his new-found acquaintances; it confirmed they'd chosen well. Thus emboldened, they removed large-bladed knives from their marsupial pouches and the taller of the two spat through his teeth, "Yeeees, we speeek a leetle anglais. Ooow you say….?.... Give us all your fucking money!!"

Nigel blinked. Intoxicated as he was, the hostile nature of this encounter was dawning upon his dulled mind. Was this 'IT'? The big whoopsie? The final curtain? Sayonara? The very reason he'd come to Andorra in the first place? As he assessed the situation, two startlingly detailed images now sprung into his usually sluggish imagination. In the first, he saw himself twenty years hence, with clarity as sure as doom. Drool was yo-yoing from the corner of his toothless mouth onto pyjamas of the type issued to the near-dead by public institutions in the UK. That which missed the pyjamas plonked onto slippers that, decades prior, had sported a spiffy Burberry tartan but were now horribly stained with a Niagara of wayward food-stuff…the pastel-coloured fodder that serves only to perpetuate a joyless existence.

As quick as it came, this image gave way to the second that, under more normal circumstances, might have seemed even more depressing: a current-day Nigel, also sporting a viscous liquid glinting its way from the corner of his mouth (quite well-toothed). But this was no drool! This was blood, coagulating rapidly in the chill of a winter's night as it descended onto the very clothes he currently wore!

Again he blinked: a choice had to be made. And quickly.

"Ah, yes, I see." he nodded. And after a thoughtful pause, "Look, I'll give you chaps all the money I've got on me…not much I'm afraid…plus my credit cards and my watch…look a Breitling that you can sell…sorry, *flog*… for, really, quite a lot of money…."

The hooded gentlemen looked confused. "What yuuuu saaayying, old man?"

With a slight puff of disgruntlement, Nigel began again, in the manner often adopted by the English abroad:

"I GIVE YOU..." (Pointing to both youths)

"...E-V-E-R-Y-THING I HAVE..." (Gesticulations of copious offerings)

"...BUT…" (Finger raised as if in judgment)

"...YOU..." (Repeat of dual-pointing)

"...MUST..." (Finger of judgment stabbing repeatedly and hyper-vigorously at his own heart)

"...KILL ME." (Drawing of finger across throat, followed by sideways flopping of head, momentary shutting of eyes and feigned loss of consciousness). "COMPRENDAAAY??"

To tell the truth, life had not been exactly a cake walk for the two lads, now somewhat unnerved by the terms with which they'd been presented. Sadly, even a brief summary of the history of the Roma people (*'Gens de Voyage'*; 'Travellers'; 'Gypsies') and their wanderings over the centuries, their superstitions and customs, is beyond the scope of our story. Suffice to say it's no joke being a Roma youth in a France ridden with unemployment of a scale and obstinacy only achievable through decades of social engineering designed to resolve their plight but achieving the opposite.

A grubby palm is raised to Nigel's face, as if to say, '*Un moment, s'il vous plait, Monsieur.*' After a quick conference in which to confirm what they just heard, the two youths......

OK, stop everything. Let's test your faith, or lack thereof, in human nature. Please choose one of the following endings:

Nigel is immediately and viciously stabbed to death - Brutus himself would have winced. Later at the French border, a customs officer, absorbed by a licentious text on his phone from his girlfriend, ignores the perps, who drive right on by, free as birds. They get over 10,000 euros for the Breitling. Quite a bit less for the cigarettes.

Or

Having distracted them with a mesmerizing line of B.S., Nigel grabs the two lads by their knife-hands and, with an upward-rotating move learned in his SAS training prior to deployment to Belfast in the '70's, drives each lad's knife up through their respective nasal passages into their cranial cavities, killing them instantly and simultaneously. Nigel lights a cigarette, hands as steady as a rock, and saunters off home.

Or

Same as B above, but the dead bodies over which Nigel steps en route to the bar remind him of why he came to Andorra in the first place. Stooping, he works one of the knives loose from the face in which it is embedded and turns it on himself, ceremoniously jabbing it up under his sternum and waggling it around until he too succumbs, flopping down on the bodies of his victims. Heavy snow begins to fall. The deeply-frozen corpses are not discovered until the spring thaw, by which time mysterious glacial forces and the attentions of feral dogs have transmogrified the trio into an intertwined morass of naked male intimacy sufficiently off-colour in nature to fuel ex-pat cocktail-party conversation in Andorra for years to come.

Actually none of the above is exactly correct. Having established that Nigel's proposal was made in deadly earnest and that therefore he was dangerously insane, the two louts freaked, running off empty-handed. So spooked were they at this accursed encounter and, raised as they were among Romany superstitions that upon reaching their van panting and frothing at the mouth like hunted beasts, they hurled their contraband onto the roadside and fled the country, un-assailed by the authorities.

Nigel's remaining days were many. Indeed, with so much time on his hands, he started giving it away to anyone who asked for it. A helping hand here, an errand run there...pretty soon he was so immersed in other people's lives he'd all but forgotten that he'd come to Andorra to end his own. But, in the end, that 'IT' moment awaits us all. In a small cemetery in the orderly town of La Massana, nestled in one of Andorra's northern valleys, Nigel's memorial plaque reads exactly as he came, over time, to wish it:

"Nigel Craig
1929 - 2013
Lived long. Much missed."

Author's Note: some of the above was inspired by a guy I worked for in New York who, while descending in an elevator alone, late at night, from his office on the 77th floor of the Chrysler Building, encountered a drug-crazed, recently-terminated mailroom clerk wielding a box cutter who entered at the 45th floor and was out for revenge from anyone in a suit. Such was my boss' compassion for humanity and evenness of temperament that, by the time they'd reached the ground floor, the pair were on first-name terms and, to aid his erstwhile assailant, my boss bought the box cutter for what even the lad volunteered was an embarrassing – but no less welcome - sum of money.

A couple named Peter and Sal
Chose to go skiing at Pal
But at the nice cafeteria
They drank too much sangria
And missed the gondola's last call

#6 FESTIVAL

HOLY WEEK & EASTER

Holy Week traditionally starts on Palm Sunday when people go to Mass to commemorate Jesus' triumphant entry into Jerusalem when palm fronds are said to have been strewn in his path. Today, up to the age of 12, godmothers present their godsons with *palmons* and their goddaughters with *palmes*. The *palmons* of the boys are large, simple pieces of palm leaf or a sprig of laurel whereas the girls' *palmes* require considerable skill to weave into intricate designs. The children take their palms to church to be blessed. On Good Friday a vigil is held in Andorra's churches. And on Easter Sunday a special Mass is said. There is also an Anglican Easter Sunrise Service held at the Coll de la Botella, incredibly moving on a clear day – not such fun in a blizzard.

As mentioned before, Andorra has a special cake for almost every major feast day and Easter is no exception. The word 'mona' comes from the Moroccan term meaning 'gift' and, traditionally, at Easter time godfathers give a Mona to their godchildren. This dates back to the 15th century. The Mona normally features eggs, one for each year of the child's life. They are also a symbol of the end of 40 days of Lenten austerity. Originally the cake was in the shape of a ring with the eggs perched along the rim but today they are more like a Victoria sandwich cake filled with apricot jam and topped off with Disney figures or Barcelona football players and flamboyant, brightly-coloured 'feathers'.

Bakers from Catalonia alone expect to sell 600,000 of these cakes by the end of Holy Week.

Caramelles are popular Easter songs typical of Catalonia. Originally, back in the 16th century, they were sung to celebrate the good news of the resurrection of Jesus Christ. Nowadays they include many secular songs. Rather like carol singers, Caramellaires (the singers) go round the streets in groups, often accompanied by instrumentalists. They stop under the balconies of friends and neighbours to sing to them. Then they pass up a basket bedecked with ribbons and attached to the end of a long pole so that those on the balcony can make donations of eggs or sausages or money. These donations are used by the group for a communal meal, either that evening or a few days later. In some places the singers also dance between songs.

SUMMER

On the track I met
A bull; a gentleman, he
quite ignored my fear.

Valerie Rymarenko

A WALK ON THE DARK SIDE

Of witches, witchcraft, and other strange matters

by J. P. Wood

On a sunny day, walk through the main thoroughfares of Andorra, snow-capped mountains postcard clichés against an innocent sky. Shops overspill with designer clothes and state-of-the art electronics while people clutching mobile phones to their ears gaze out from internet-dazzled eyes.

Old Andorra seems a myth and witchcraft nothing but a clutch of old wives' tales.

However, on a dark and stormy winter's day or, in high summer, when skies are riven by lightning, go into the mountains; or seek out the villages and visit the churches, squat defences against the powers of darkness. Look up at the sad and sombre face of the many carvings of the Virgin instinct with the knowledge of Good and Evil; or gaze into the sad, wise eyes of her Child. Then look behind them at the reredos. Saints and biblical scenes are watched over by God the Father. Yes, he's the jolly, naughty-looking, rosy-cheeked fellow at the top. Doesn't he seem infinitely more of a pagan deity, a cheerful Bacchus or playful Saturn?

This ancient landscape was once, is maybe still, a centre of witchcraft and sorcery. Prepare yourself for a journey through the Andorra of *les Bruixes*, the witches, of *la Bruixeria,* sorcery.

Let me show you the dark side.

****

Traces of man and his artefacts date from nine millennia before Christ. Little is documented before the twelfth century; much is superstition and folk memory. Druids, animists and polytheist Romans may have performed their rites here but few traces remain.

Except the rocks which tell a history all of their own. Great stones exist in Sornas, Ordino, La Massana, Canillo, near the church of Sant Joan de Caselles, in Andorra la Vella, Les Escaldes and Sant Julià. Many are incised with rudimentary figures of man and beast, both sometimes horned, accompanied by more abstract circles, triangles, lozenges and of course pentacles, most arcane of shapes. Some of the drawings are thought to date to the Bronze Age. Above *Can Diumenge* they say there is a rock carved into the face of a lion or lion-man staring defensively out across the valleys.

Most famous of all is the *Roc de les Bruixes de Prats,* Canillo; the drawings on the *Roc de les Bruixes* of Andorra have been erased by time. Witches of both sexes were supposed to congregate at these rocks for their satanic orgies. Research, however, has shown that the *Roc de les Bruixes de Prats* is covered with graffiti depicting foot and horse warriors. The shape of the helmets worn by the soldiers dates the graffiti somewhere between the end of the 13th and the beginning of the 14th centuries. These may be a depiction of the battles between the Co-Princes, Count of Foix, Roger Bernat III and the Bishop of Seu d'Urgell, Pere d'Urg.

In 16th and 17th century Europe there was something of a Witchy-Gate. Witches were persecuted in France, Germany, England, and, by the monstrous Inquisition, in Spain and the Low Countries. The Pyrenees were noted as a centre of witchcraft and sorcery. A prime meeting place was Andorra, particularly the exquisitely named lake, *Engolasters* or Star-swallower.

If you go up there now, you will find the calm and shallow waters of the reservoir for the parish, trout suspended in its clear green depths or gasping at its edge when ice covers the waters and the tree-lined shores look like the best of Christmas cards. During summer storms when the lake reflects shades of purple and indigo, the place takes on a more sombre aspect and it is not so hard to believe the legend that on the Eve of *Sant Joan*, (Saint John's Eve), all the witches of the Pyrenees congregated here, crying out as they flew through the air, 'Follow me, this way, this way,' in voices as shrill as birds. And that, once gathered here under influences of their Master, they danced their lubricious dances until dawn.

It is said that certain rash humans wishing to take part in the orgy were transformed by the witches into black cats which clung howling to the backs of their whirling, prancing, spinning hosts; an interesting image.

A version of the legend reports that the humans awoke, exhausted and bruised, but with no memory of the orgy; another declares that the population of black cats in Andorra exponentially increased.

Some legends speak of witches in a more positive way, giving them a role in protecting the freedom of this tiny country from the invading and rapacious *Forasters,* the outsiders. In *The White Lady of Auvinyà*, the eponymous White Lady protects her country against the marauding bishop. *The 'Legend of the Three Soldiers'* is a story of a witch, ugly, harsh, and unloved. A beautiful, sweet, young woman comes to live with her. Under the girl's influence, the witch becomes generous and kind. She gives hospitality to three deserters, who reward her kindness by raping and murdering the girl. The soldiers are *Forasters* and the witch uses her occult powers to punish them. In *The Ravine of the Demon*, the Devil is a foreigner who is prevented by a pious Andorran shepherd from making off with his Andorran sinners.

The patron saint of Andorra is the Virgin of Meritxell, whose name, some say, derives from *Mereig*, or midday, the solar and moral opposite of midnight. The role of the Virgin is curiously similar to that of the good witches. She, too, is called upon to protect Andorra from foreign threat as can be heard in the hymn sung to Her every 8th September when pilgrims from the Valleys flock to celebrate her Day. Part of the anthem reads thus:

VERSE
You watch over the Valleys
And as our Queen
You protect the faith of Andorrans
From the poison of heresy
Which can never enter here

CHORUS
If war should threaten us
Your sacred mantle
And your prodigious power
Will protect this land

From its terrible torment
And repel the enemy

The Mother Church did not perceive witches in quite the same way. The number of covens grew until, in the year 1595, the Bishop of La Seu d'Urgell called upon Don Francisco Arevalo de Zauso, the Grand Inquisitor of Barcelona, to sort out these pestilential creatures.

The French Co-Prince, Henry IV, was infuriated by this action of the Inquisition which he saw as part of the machinery of State rather than the Church. He sent a letter asserting that no justice could be administered in Andorra, other than the justice permitted to the *Veguers* (legal representatives of the Co-Princes). Thus the Tribunal of the *Corts*, the civil court of Andorra, presided over by the two *Veguers*, took over the righteous battle against sorcery and Andorran witches were preserved from some of the more extreme miseries of their Spanish counterparts.

Not that their lives were precisely blissful.

Accusations of witchcraft were brought by the 'worthies of the parish'. Witches or supposed witches suffered tortures, including suspension by hands or feet, with weights added, and beatings. Generally the extent of the torture was limited to the length of an "Ave" or a "Pater Noster". It should be noted that torments could be repeated until justice had what it required; an admission of sorcery, a recantation of the Devil.

There were no great witch-hunts, no *autos-da-fé*, and compared to witches in other parts of Europe, those of Andorra were treated relatively lightly, although as punishment was often monetary, the people, poor as they were, perhaps did not see it that way.

For example, in March, 1629, Pere Perot, of Andorra la Vella, sworn Nuncio of the valleys and Procurator Fiscal of the court, demanded that Pere Poncernalt Mora, Episcopal *Batlle*, confiscate the goods of different persons accused of witchcraft, in accordance with the agreement that the men and women accused of this crime should pay 25 Barcelonan pounds to the Fiscal. The other punishments were confiscation of goods, and exile. Some, but not so many, suffered the death penalty.

Who were these witches? Many were healers, old and solitary women, single or widowed, usually ugly, unloved and unneeded, except on those occasions when their neighbours, unable to afford the cost of a doctor, came to them for country remedies. Often, these sad crones had a small piece of land, a cottage, or maybe a few beasts. The neighbours, 'the worthies of the parish', coveting these meagre goods, would accuse them of witchcraft. Since there were many accusers and few defenders, it was simple enough to bring about the confiscation and expropriation of these desirables. Sometimes too, simple minds, unable to come to terms with deaths in the family, explained their tragedies by witchcraft, and then looked around for a scapegoat.

Several witches were accused of poisoning or otherwise murdering their neighbours or the neighbours' beasts. The murder of small children was especially popular since the fat and organs of innocent infants were considered essential to create the unguent necessary for flying.

Generally speaking, the witches were supposed to have entered the houses of their victims through windows opened for them by their Lord and Master, The Evil One. However, most of the witches seemed to have been more ill-wishing than demonic although, under duress, some admitted to sexual congress with Satan, usually of a perverse nature. Jean-Francis Galinier-Pallerola makes the point that such uneducated, impoverished souls would hardly have knowledge of esoteric matters. More likely, he concludes, the ideas were unconsciously transmitted to them by their interrogators, more educated but no less superstitious men.

Look at Maria Galoxa, aka Palancro whose trial for witchcraft took place between 1st September, 1621 and 11th October, 1621 before the two *Veguers*. Hers was a classic case; a widow, 58 years of age, she was accused of witchcraft and poisoning. There were eight witnesses.

You can imagine the scene, five men and three women from the Parish of Ordino gathered around the authoritative *Veguers*, nervousness and guilt adding a shrill self-righteousness to their accusations, some of which reached well back into the past.

Two witnesses, perhaps overcome with that guilt, speak very vaguely of Maria's ill reputation.

"Ah yes," declares another, "she poisoned my son".

"And my wife," cries a second. "She poisoned my wife." He points towards another witness. "And I'm certain, as God is my witness, that she murdered this man's daughter."

"Aye," chimes in the third. "And her ill-wishing has murdered my beasts, and my wife."

"Ah!" moans a woman. "My daughter, my son, and the grandchild and him only ten months old, all gone, all gone."

"Just like my bairn, so young," sobs another wrapping her arm round her neighbour's shoulders. "And then my strong boy, already a help on the farm." She glares around at the others. "He came with me into that witch's kitchen, and as we crossed the threshold, he cried out and told me his foot pained him." She pauses and shudders. "And then he sickened and died."

A man present, and hereto silent, nods sombrely. "I was at the funeral," says he. "And I heard the foul witch speak."

"What did she say?" demands the *Veguer*.

In a shrill mimicry of poor Maria, the man replies. "I have seen what I wished to see."

At first Maria denied the accusations and denied any knowledge of witchcraft. But when she was beaten, her confessions went beyond that of which she was accused. She admitted being involved with other witches, of making a pact with the Devil, of having intercourse with the Devil 'from behind' and of having obeyed his commands to trample on the Cross and to deny God, the Virgin and the Saints. She admitted to having taken part in a black Mass. After a second bout of torture, she confirmed her confession and named others involved.

Maria was one of those sad creatures sentenced to death by hanging. Before her death, she withdrew her confessions and attempted to exonerate all those she had named.

The Church in Andorra virtuously persecuted witches until well into the 17th century. It is curious, then, to see some of the patron saints chosen by that same Church to protect the country's lovely Romanesque churches.

In Canillo, near the Sanctuary of the Virgin of Meritxell there is a delightful 12th century church dedicated to the most unconventional Sant Serni, or Sant Sadurni, a pagan god, protector of the crops and harvest.

This same god appears in the church of Ordino and protects another church, Sant Serni of Nagol perched high on the slopes above Sant Julià.

The church of Ordino enjoys two fascinating patrons, Sant Corneli and Sant Cebrià. Sant Corneli or Cornelius was said to be part of an occult sect which studied arcane mysteries and he was believed, through his own powers, to have razed a Roman temple and destroyed a pagan image. Sant Cebrià or Cyprian was reputed to be a Carthaginian magus who wrote, amongst other things, the celebrated *Grimoria de Magia*, a study of the occult.

At the church of Sant Joan de Caselles, you will see a mural in which the soldier, Longinas and the centurion, Stephaton are dominated by the Sun and the Moon, far from traditional Christian emblems.

As in many Catholic countries, stone crosses mark the roads and the fields. Some have queer legends attached to them. In the pastures near Canillo there is a representation of the gothic 'Cross with Seven Branches' mentioned in the legend of that name. (The original cross is in the Casa del Comú of Canillo and can be visited, with permission). Above Prats, is a Cross reputed to have been erected by

Carlemany (Charlemagne) but was more likely to have been placed there to protect the fields and pastures. Old houses have crosses above or next to the main doorway which serve similar purposes. On the exterior of the church at Ordino, there is a small structure with four pillars, one for each cardinal point, designeded to protect the building from storms or from the ill will of witches.

Today things have changed. The grip of the church on the everyday business of the country has weakened, and no-one, but no-one, believes in the occult.

Or do they?

Scan the pages of the magazine '7 Dies' (Seven Days). You will find advertisements for those who will tell your fortune, cast your horoscope, avert evil. A friend of mine whose neighbour has grown wealthy on this business says that it is not only the poor and simple who consult him. I wonder, do these modern soothsayers use the same complex astrological system as that detailed in the fragment of medieval manuscript known as the 'Tencar' where not only the person, but each part of the body is governed by a different astrological sign.

I heard a tale of a factory employing mostly women from Galicia, Andalucía and Portugal. There was a girl from the south, a gypsy, who married a boy whose mother didn't take kindly to gypsy blood in the family. The girl sickened and was unable to recover, although when she spent a few weeks with her family in Spain she got better. Returning to her husband, she sickened again. Encouraged by the women at work, she consulted a good-hearted fellow-worker known to be a white witch. This woman lit a candle and when it was burnt out, examined the form the melted wax had taken and declared the girl to be under a black spell, no doubt ordered and paid for by her mother-in-law. She also claimed to know those involved in the casting of the spell and said that she would take things in hand.

The gypsy girl recovered, and it is said that two of the three involved in casting the spell are dead, while the other one is ailing. Of the mother-in-law's health, I can tell you nothing.

Let me leave you with these words carved on a stone monument to the Catalan priest and poet, Mossén J. Verdaguer. It is his own lovely poem and I believe it applies to the entirety of this enchanting and mysterious country.

Les Valls de Ordino y d'Inclés
son més plenes d'harmonia
de somni y misteris

The Valleys of Ordino and of Incles
are quite full of harmony
and of dreams and mysteries.

OUTDOOR ANDORRA

by Iain Woolward

Andorra is the most mountainous country in the world. Unlike, say, Nepal, which has extensive flat bits, Andorra has hardly any. Nearly all of its 181 square miles (constituting the 195th largest country on earth) are mountainous. A smattering of towns and generally andorrable (couldn't resist) villages nestle at the foot of steep-sided valleys carved by the millennia out of the south facing slopes of the eastern Pyrenees. The main town, and, incidentally, Europe's highest capital, sensibly called Andorra La Vella, sits on relatively flat land where two river valleys meet, but most of Andorra's settlements had to be hewn out of rock-slides and cliff-sides.

In summer the upper reaches of Andorran mountainsides constitute a wide-open, un-fenced playground for any who hanker for height. Some folks ascend as far as they can on four wheels; others descend as fast as they can on two. Then there are the hikers and climbers.

Some find it weird how others like to slog, grim-faced and panting, up mountains. The tougher the better. For a particularly keen minority, climbing doesn't seem to even start to be any fun until lives are being put on the line. To that end they flock to the likes of Everest where, masked and cramponed, they politely shuffle around the dead and dying just to get up as high as they can, hoping to get down in one piece. This is no exaggeration. I have first-hand reports from the first woman to have scaled Everest from opposing sides of the mountain – Cathy O'Dowd, a neighbour in Andorra. Of over 248 people who have died on Everest so far, a whole bunch are still up there, frozen in time. Helicopters are no good; they poop out well short of the top. And nobody en route to or from the summit messes around with corpses for fear of becoming one. However, a few expeditions have been devoted exclusively to clearing away the ghostly remains of some of those in whose footsteps so many have climbed…at least on the way up.

Climbing in Andorra isn't like that. It's just plain pleasant. Don't get me wrong: the Andorran Pyrenees are proper mountains, but your chances of dying on one are about the same as being struck by lightning – which is how almost all the few fatalities on these mountains occur….at least in summer. (Skiing is a different matter entirely). Ironically, the more pleasant the conditions in the morning, the greater the risk of lightning in the afternoon. When the general weather is moving in from the south, sun-warmed air rises up the mountainsides in the late morning reaching its 'dew point' in the early afternoon. Clouds form. Big clouds. Things can get pretty interesting shortly thereafter. However, most days Andorra offers memorable mountaineering and hill-walking for the sane, level-headed majority who have no desire to put lives on the line. Why grope your way along some knife-edged Andean ridge in a blinding blizzard, roped to some guy just so that he doesn't get lonely falling to his death (and yours)? In Andorra, you can drive the average family saloon to a spectacular 'col' and still have plenty of mountain left on which to make like a mountaineer. Why risk having your blue, lifeless, space-suited body stare out in perpetuity from a Himalayan ice wall when you can ascend, say, Andorra's Alt de Comapedrosa (2,942 meters) in a tee shirt and be back down by tea-time? (Sensible hill walkers will, of course, carry clothing for any eventuality and bite off only as much as their level of fitness can chew. Failure to do so can be fatal.)

Yes, if you're like me, you prefer your conquests to be on the older, more rounded side, versus those upstarts jabbing jaggedy granite fingers into the wicked-blue skies of Tibet or Chile. Andorra's mountains are among the oldest on our planet; scrubbed and smoothed by glaciers 15,000 years ago and now merely nibbled here and there by playful snow-melt. They are built of a bewildering array of ancient rocks (all conveniently comfortable under foot) squished together when Iberia was a lonely island floating around on the surface of a much mushier planet, unsure whether to seek the companionship of Africa or Europe. The entire Pyrenean range popped up about 125 million years ago, like freshly crumpled bodywork, when what is now Spain collided with what is now France. By popular account, that's 75 million years before the Himalayas even *started* their ascent. Recently some American geologists have declared that the Himalayan dating is wonky - wrong by a factor of nine. That's like saying George Washington was actually born in 192 C.E., the year Rome rid itself of the megalomaniac Commodus. But, either way and for whatever reason, the Andorran mountains are Miss Manners compared to Johnnie Rotten ranges like the Himalayas.

Another nice thing about them: should you 'summit' (using the noun as a verb is an essential part of the lingo), you will stand pressing against the breeze, staring slit-eyed at a hundred kilometre horizon, utterly alone (unless you climbed up with somebody). This makes your accomplishment seem all the more exceptional – so much better than the ill-tempered jostling now commonplace on top of many of the world's peaks. Every year about 20,000 pedestrians pace and stomp around on top of Kilimanjaro, flapping their arms for warmth. Fuji is so congested nobody keeps an exact count any more. About 250,000 a year, they reckon. On a single day in 2012, two hundred and thirty four people queued for up to two and half hours to summit Everest. "It was like MacDonald's," reported experienced mountaineer and author Graham Hoyland – which seems rather unfair to MacDonald's and the whole 'fast food' concept.

This kind of thing doesn't happen on the Andorran Pyrenees. It's entirely possible that nobody even *thought* to climb to the top of them until quite recently. Mountain life was already too hard and too short to indulge in that kind of foolery. Bear in mind that for thousands of years the Nepalese Sherpas ('eastern people') never took one unnecessary step up Chomolunga ('Everest'). Then some foreigners offered them very serious money to help conquer it. 'Conquer'? Please: the mountain has stood for 60 million years and it'll be standing, somewhat higher, on approximately the same spot long, long after our parasitic species has petered out. Meanwhile it will conspire with its own murderous micro-climate to kill almost 5% of its would-be assailants. That's a higher kill rate than the Vietcong accomplished whopping America's ass in Vietnam. Some 'conquest'! (Next door, with a lot less fanfare, Annapurna is quietly killing close to *half* of its would-be assailants).

The highest peak in Andorra is just under 3,000 meters (about 10,000 feet), but altitude isn't everything. For example, the highest mountain in the world, base-to-peak, is Hawaii's Mauna Kea. The first half of the ascent is tricky: you'll need scuba gear. But after that it's a total dawdle: you can drive to the top. Maybe drop in for a cup of coffee with the astronomers operating the observatories up there. My point is that you can stick a monster of a mountain in the middle of the Pacific Ocean and get a yawner, or pop something of more modest proportions in the middle of a continental range and get something a lot more interesting. In any case, the Pyrenees are plenty high, they look great and you don't need an aqualung *or* an oxygen tank to climb them. And, unlike the steeled watchtowers of more notorious mountains from which legends of evil have sprung, the only things to spring from the upper reaches of Andorran mountain sides are over 700 species of grass and an astonishing 1,500 species of wild flowers. Above the tree line, furry little marmots scurry about their business; below it, pine martins goof around in the, well, pines. In the distance….wait….is that the soothing toll of cow bells – a meandering melody of pastoral alpine life? High, high above us the lammergeier and griffon soar, hanging motionless upon the afternoon thermals, held aloft by wingspans as large as any in the ornithological world... If you think that's all a bunch of who-ha, I assure you it is not. Want details? Andorra is home to 17 species of mammals occupying every level of the food chain. At the top: bears, boars and wolves (2,500 of which were roaming the Spanish Pyrenees at the last count in 2006). At the bottom: the exceptionally tiny and adorably cute yellow-necked mouse. 161 species of birds have been spotted in Andorra, from among the world's largest raptors (referenced above) to 'troglodytes troglodytes' – the winter wren. (Why a tiny bird should share a name with lumbering cavepersons, the common chimpanzee and members of a 60's English rock band is unclear to me). 885 species of butterflies and moths flit about the countryside, sometimes as thick as light snowfall. And amazingly there are people – mostly English ladies - who've spent literally years on their hands and knees crawling over every one of 467,000,000 square meters of Andorra, copiously logging its flora and fauna. And those cow bells? Well, admittedly, they are as likely to grace the necks of very chunky horses as they are those of slightly leaner cows. Both munch their summers away on the upper slopes of the Andorran Pyrenees, their furry hides shimmering in the warm breeze. But don't get too attached: they're not long for this world.

One final thing: when I go to England I see signs for "English Country Walks" indicating where the public has 'Right of Way'. There's even a little person on the signposts in the act of walking - in case you either can't read or don't know how to walk. Having lived in California for a while, I find these signs refreshing. California is three times larger than England, nine hundred and four times larger than Andorra and was home to America's first National Parks. But much of the land is 'Posted' in order to give the private owner the right to relive 60's western movies scenes in which thuggish looking people brandishing Winchesters and three days of beard-growth yell, "Git offa ma land or I'll fill ya full of lead!". Then, to emphasize their point, they spit out revolting brown gobs of chewing tobacco right onto the boots of those to whom this remark is addressed.

Of course, today, the landowners are tech billionaires, bankers and movie stars. They are still entitled to blow your head off if, in their opinion, your presence represents a threat, but at least they won't spit on your shoes. The remaining land is 'public' in that you and your fellow tax-payers have paid for it....you co-own it. But you still have to pay a fee to get on most of it and, even if you don't, it's regulated up the gazoo. All this is 'Mars' to Andorra's 'Venus' (or is it the other way round?). In Andorra over 80% of the land is open, free, do-what-the-hell-you-like land.... with the exception of cutting down trees. You can hike on it, bike on it and walk your dog on it. For a couple of weeks a year, you can shoot some things on it. There are no notices yelling, 'PRIVATE LAND. KEEP OFF!' or 'STAY ON THE PATH!". Only some Hobbit-styled sign posts pointing to similarly-styled villages to be encountered should you wish to wander that way. There are 54 well-maintained marked trails from which to choose, varying from loops of a few kilometres to a 100 kilometre trek around the entire country. High altitude routes are interspersed with 26 mountain huts complete with water supply and cooking fireplaces. Everything is free and unsullied.

Andorrans are close to their land. They really do own it. They take responsibility for it. They look after it. They love it. I think you will too.

Andorrans who climb the Pyrenees
Ascend with commendable ease
But, by the time they get down
(Usually via Ordino town)
Most are on hands and knees.

SHAVE TO THE IRON

A glimpse into Andorran Cuisine and where best to find it

by Alexandra Grebennikova

A word to the wise: if your mind is set on enjoying Andorran cuisine, it helps to be able to read the menu! Let me explain why.

One beautiful summer evening, my Andorran husband and I went out for a meal in a restaurant located in the northern part of the Andorran valleys. I always say that in Andorra everybody knows everybody else: of course it can't really be true. We ended up in a place where nobody knew us. My husband looks slightly foreign, and so do I (a blue-eyed blonde about 5'8" tall), so a smiling waiter brought us a menu in English. We opened it - and froze. "Shave to the Iron," read my husband. "And here, look: Octopus to the Galician One". Whatever else was in there, I do not recall, but clearly Google translator had made a particularly bad job of it.

While we were having a ball with this delicious sample of internet-based translation, a particularly distinguished-looking British couple arrived and sat at the table next to ours. They received the menu, presumably the same one we were reading, opened it - looked at each other in alarm… and left. Now if they had just learnt a few culinary phrases in Catalan all would have been well and Catalan is such a musical language too!

We stayed on and gave it a try. "Shave to the Iron" turned

out to be grilled monkfish, and the Galician-one's octopus was simply superb! Which means, once again, that it might be a good idea to know what you are looking for from the very start, as the childish faith of the local restaurant owners in automated translators doesn't mean they can't cook: more often than not, they can, but unless you know how to recognise the names of the dishes on a Catalan menu, chances are you will end up eating pizza and *spaghetti Carbonara* more often than you expected. However if you do want pizza, may I recommend *La Cantina* in la Plaça de les Arcades in Andorra la Vella, my personal favourite, just in front of an excellent wine bar called *L'Alternativa* and surrounded by other quaint bars and restaurants in the heart of the old town: *El Faisà*, *Versailles*, *Crostó, Ca la Conxita* and many more.

In order for you to judge how much credibility my opinions on food deserve, I should tell you that I grew up in an industrial Russian city. This means, I was born in a place where cuisine as such did not exist, there was just cooking, and you usually cooked whatever you could find in the shops. What you could find in the shops was usually vegetables, which ensured we had a nutritious and healthy diet, but also that sometimes we settled for macaroni no cheese (and no sauce) or a salad made of everything you found in the fridge. Maybe a similar situation was the starting point of many national cuisines, or else we wouldn't be eating snails or pig's feet.

If you *are* into snails, you certainly should try *Cargols a la Llauna* at *Can Manel*, in Andorra la Vella, a local classic. I also find their *Canelons de l'Àvia* (grandmother's cannelloni) absolutely delicious.

The old saying, we are what we eat, might be true, and our memories of the places we visit are always connected to the food we try there, to the wine we drink, to new tastes and flavours, smells and textures. I love Andorran food. When I go away for more than a fortnight, I start missing it the way one misses home; that's why I hope you will come to visit us, and that you will like the things we cook.

For starters, you could try a *trinxat* (a dish of mashed potatoes and cabbage and smoky bacon), *calçots* (giant spring onions with a Romesco sauce), a salad made of fresh spring dandelion leaves, or *xicoies* (don't worry, they know how to avoid the toxic ones), homemade pâtés, *Coca de recapte* (the Catalan version of a pizza) or grilled vegetables (*verdures grillades*). You might also be offered the ever-popular *Pa amb tomaquet*, toasted bread rubbed with tomato, garlic and salt, with a bit of olive oil. This, without the tomatoes, was the traditional breakfast of the shepherds when grazing their flocks in the mountains. It can come accompanied by excellent cheeses (the neighbouring frontier town of La Seu d'Urgell is one of Catalonia's most reputed centres of cheese production). Local charcuterie (*Embotits*) is also a must, and I especially recommend *fuet* (thin, dried pork sausage) and *llonganissa*.

As a main course, I would choose *Truita a l'andorrana*, or Andorran-style trout, famous in the region since the Middle Ages. You could also try *civet d'isard*, a chamois stew: and it might be a good idea to order one of these for two or three, as the servings are copious. *Civets* are stews made of chamois, wild boar or mountain goat: they are very good at *El Celler d'en Toni* (Andorra la Vella) and *Borda Raubert* (La Massana). Another one of the local specialities is *Carns a la pedra*: meat cooked on a hot stone. *Espatlla de corder*, shoulder of lamb, prepared in different ways, is usually a star dish too.

As to desserts, it seems to me that fresh cottage cheese with honey (*mel i mató*) or crème brulée (*crema andorrana*, also known as *crema catalana*) would cater to most tastes. Another alternative is *el postre de músic*, dried fruits and nuts with sweet *Muscatel* wine that the inns used to give to wandering minstrels to see them on their way.

Apart from typically Andorran restaurants and the tourist-oriented "no man's land" of eateries that fill the main streets, international cuisine is also well represented in Andorra. There are some excellent Russian restaurants (for example, *El Cresper* in Encamp), two or three pretty decent Chinese places, Argentinian, Thai, Indian, Mexican and Japanese cuisine, British pubs and Swiss fondue bars.

Still I prefer the local dishes where they use a lot of fresh vegetables and olive oil (why don't you try *escalivada*, which is baked aubergines and peppers), various kinds of legumes, lots of different mushrooms and meat (usually pork, veal, poultry and lamb).

Andorran meat and potatoes are a matter of pride to the country, which means, that in a traditional Andorran restaurant, it isn't easy to get a vegetarian option: they seem to think it is a must to add something meat-related such as ham to any vegetable-based dish. (I was told this dated back to the Inquisition days in Spain when, to test if Jews and Moors had truly converted to Christianity, they made them eat pork!) If you are just looking for some Spanish-style tapas to go with your beer, try *patates braves* (potatoes in a spicy tomato sauce) that they serve almost everywhere or Spanish omelettes with potatoes and aubergines and cured *Jabugo* ham.

When you visit Andorra as I hope you will, you can ask me any further questions about places where you can eat. Just stroll up and down the main street four or five times and observe the passers-by. I'll be the 5'8" tall blonde with a big smile. After all this is a really small country. And if, for any unforeseen reason, you can't find me there, just try one of the restaurants I have recommended. Apart from the ones I've already mentioned, my favourites are *La Borda Xica* in La Massana (make sure you book in advance, it's very small), *La Torrada* in Xixerella (most vegetables come from their own vegetable garden), and *La Borda Vella* in Encamp (a traditional country home converted into a beautiful restaurant). For a cheap and good-quality lunchtime option, try the *Bon Racó* in Santa Coloma or *Big Ben* in Escaldes. My bet is, you won't be disappointed.

There was an old man from St Julia
Whose life was rather peculiar
On Tuesdays he dined
On Fridays he wined
And on Sunday he sang 'Hallelujah'!

#7 FESTIVAL

23rd & 24th JUNE: SANT JOAN & THE SUMMER SOLSTICE

The Eve and Festival of Sant Joan (pronounced Jo-won) is held on the Summer Solstice when the sun reaches its zenith. (Interestingly, for the Catalans, this is considered the beginning of summer whereas in the UK it is known as Midsummer's Eve.) Arguably, it is Catalonia's and Andorra's favourite festival. Starting at sunset on 23rd June, it lasts right through the night till the dawn of the 24th with open-air parties in the mountains or on the beaches of Catalonia, while rockets and bonfires keep the night alive.

In ancient times the sun symbolised fertility and wealth; the stronger the sun, the more fecund the crops and livestock and the more prosperous the people. A mass of bonfires was thought to boost the sun's power. So, before Health and Safety came to douse the fun, fires were lit everywhere: in all the side streets and little squares. Lovers were even encouraged to hold hands and leap over the flames seven times to boost fertility!

The 'Mother' Flame of Canigó. Mount Canigó, 2,784m high, is sacred to the Catalan peoples rather as Mt Fuji is to the Japanese. Situated just across the frontier in the French Pyrenees, it used to be part of North Catalonia. In 1955 a bonfire was lit on the peak of Canigó from which torches were brought down to light the bonfires for Sant Joan. Ever since then the 'mother' flame has been kept alive in a kitchen near Perpignan. Each year, on the 22nd June, a new bonfire is lit on Canigó using this flame and young people come from all over Catalonia and Andorra on bikes, even on skateboards to carry back the 'daughter' flames to light the village bonfires. It is reckoned that over 90% of Sant Joan bonfires, maybe 3,000 in all, are lit from the fire on Mt. Canigó.

Each parish in Andorra has their *fallaires*, or firebrand-runners and each parish takes it in turn to host The Flame.

Another essential feature of Sant Joan is the *falles* **or fire brands**. Said to originate with Charlemagne as a weapon of war, they were once made from the bark of white birch, dried over time and then set alight. Today, with the aim of protecting the trees, the *falles* are made from more environmentally friendly wads of thick white paper held together by chicken wire attached to the end of a long chain. Once darkness falls, the *fallaires* set them alight and spin these flaming 'balls' around their heads creating the impression of great wheels of fire coming down the mountains, purifying the air and driving out evil spirits.

Finally, as with most self-respecting Catalan festivals, Sant Joan has its own special pastry with a glazed, bread-like base, often covered with beaten egg white or 'custard' and topped off with chopped, brightly coloured fruits.

AND THEN THERE'S SUMMER

by Clare Allcard

To most people Andorra is synonymous with winter: skiing, white peaks, shopping, cheap ciggies and booze. But an Andorran summer has as much to offer and more.

Take the climate. With global warming it's becoming almost impossible to wander the Spanish beaches at lunch time – and in your bedroom at night, unless you're being chilled by the air conditioning, you stifle in the heat. Andorra also provides hot summer days but, outside the city centre, the nights are usually a delicious 15°C. Like sipping cool water.

Naturlandia: For those aged 0 to a 100

As you cross the border from Spain almost the first thing to catch your eye is a huge sign advertising Naturlandia; Andorra's theme park.

To be honest it wasn't until several years after it opened that curiosity finally sent me up the long, winding road to investigate. Open year-round, Naturlandia is home to the Tobotronc, the world's longest toboggan run set on rails. It's like a vast fairground ride as it hurtles down through 5.3kms/3.3miles of alternating woodland and spectacular views. It was the Tobotronc that finally lured me up there. I had to give it a try.

The first time I rode it I played it all wrong. Firmly strapped into the plastic *luge* and with the brakes permanently on, the rider controls the thrills by taking the brakes *off* on the straights and then leaves the machine to brake automatically on the sharp, tilting bends. Or so I thought. The problem was the bends. As the G forces yank you outwards and downwards; if you let the brakes take control, the scary parts simply last even longer.

It was a gentle Singaporean who set me straight. "Oh no, you mustn't brake on the bends, Clare! Provided there's no one right ahead of you, you just keep the brakes off from top to bottom!" I tried it a second time – and it works! Amazing sensation! And ever so good for boosting the heart rate!

For those who like their excitement higher off the ground, Naturlandia also has Aitrekk, the longest Sky Trail in Europe. Built out of wood and wire and with three grades of difficulty, it rises to 13.5m/44ft and provides thrills for both adults and children – all wearing safety harnesses of course!

This year I drove up with a 100-year-old friend (said by the attendant to be their oldest visitor ever), to investigate the upper reaches of the park. Spread out across a plateau at 2,000m/6,500ft there's a children's petting farm in one corner. Here they can stroke rabbits and pat goats or, in season, tickle the bellies of little piglets that have learnt to roll over to have their buttons counted. And then there's the Animal Park. This houses examples of the Pyrenees' main indigenous species, some of which are sadly rare nowadays. Large, wooded enclosures are spread around the edge of the plateau with walkways and viewing platforms for visitors. Pushed round in a wheelchair for convenience, my friend was greatly entertained by a roly-poly brown bear as it ambled nonchalantly down between the trees and a wolf sunning itself, stretched full length in a golden patch of light that had penetrated its woodland home.

I have to say the concrete walkway was pretty rough for wheelchairs and the lavatory for the disabled half way round the circuit was up such a steep ramp that I am quite sure no wheelchair users – unless perhaps Olympians - could reach it on their own.

Visit   http://www.naturlandia.ad/activitats/estiu   for information on the myriad other activities available to create a stimulating day out for all ages in the clean mountain air. And Naturlandia lies 1,200m above, and 8km away from the nearest town, Sant Julià, giving you the bonus of driving one of Andorra's most spectacular roads to get there.

VallNord and Grand Valira ski stations also offer a wealth of summer activities: pony trekking, archery, zip-chord rides, go-carts, bouncy castles, quad bikes, the lot.

Romanesque Riches

You really need to come in summer to make the most of Andorra's treasure-trove of Romanesque and pre-Romanesque churches. In July and August many are opened to visitors. Most date from the 11th and 12th century and some minute ones, high up in the summer pastures, were built even earlier. Some, now half hidden in the back streets of modern towns, were once at the very heart of village life.

From June through September there are tourist buses that follow various routes showing some of the best of Andorra's scenery and including entrance tickets to the museums and churches visited on the way. All the buses provide English audio guides.

Altitude Training

Are you one of the many thousands of people in the western world who take part in runs/walks/triathlons to raise money for charity? Want to reach the starting line in 'peak' condition? Andorra could be the training ground for you. For the really serious bods, Soldeu, at over 1,800 metres, is the ideal altitude for the professionals. (For centuries it was the highest, permanently occupied village in the Pyrenees.) But all Andorra's higher parishes offer training opportunities for the keen amateur. After a morning's workout either on foot or bike (Andorra's mountain passes are often used by the Tours de France, España and Catalunya for high climb finishes), head off into the Alpine meadows for a picnic. Or check out the Pireneu Mountain Club. They often organize weekend excursions led by well-informed guides who know all the most interesting places to go.

Or you could tie your training in with one of Andorra's many high altitude races. There are walks and runs for all abilities including families. If you're working towards a marathon why not start with a Travessa, a race over the mountains from one parish to the next? Or sign up for the easier stages of the Andorra Ultra Trail: a 10km walk or a 42.5km, 83km or 112km mountain race. Then build up, over the years, to the granddaddy of them all: the Ronda dels Cims (Circuit of the Peaks) said by some to be the world's toughest 100 miler with 13,500m elevation gains across 15 summits between 2,400m and 3,000m high. The route circles the whole country, covers 170kms, offers stunning scenery and lasts a maximum of 62 hours. Not for the faint hearted. To qualify, you not only have to produce certificates of health and insurance but proof that you've already finished a 100km race with over 4,500m of elevation gain. Seems to me maybe a sanity check is also called for!

See http://andorraultratrail.com/

Mountain biking.

In recent years Andorra's Vallnord Bike Park has become a European and World centre for mountain bike championships. With its 1,000m height difference and 40 km of downhill tracks, it hosted a World Cup competition in 2013 and, in 2015, successfully played host to the UCI World Championships: downhill, cross country and trial.

But the bike park is not the exclusive domain of world champions. With its downhill circuits, a wood park, cross country and 4X it offers circuits for all ages and abilities including a wood park for 6-10 year olds. There is also a bike trial area designed by world champion, Xavi Casas and a Mountain Bike school run by a professional team of trainers giving beginners and advanced classes to individuals and groups.

After that, why not relax every muscle in your body with a session at the Caldea?

The Caldea

This is one of Andorra's main tourist attractions both summer and winter. Many think its glistening glass spire (see the book cover) is a modernistic cathedral and in a way it is – for the devotion to personal pampering. Situated in the parish of Escaldes-Engordany (Escaldes means hot water), local hot springs feed into what is southern Europe's biggest spa centre.

Before visiting Caldea, take a look at the following website. It explains what you're supposed to do at each installation. (Children have to be 1.20m/4ft or over to enter the facilities.)

http://www.hola-andorra.com/caldea/guidei.html

The great secret at Caldea is to take it easy. Another secret in high season is to get there early, say 10am, as the place crowds up later in the day.

I personally hate getting into cold water. (Mind you not so keen on getting into hot water either!) So let me share with you my ideal circuit. And remember, relax, enjoy each installation before wending your way to the next. You've got 3 hours, plenty of time.

From the big indoor lagoon climb up the steps to those weird looking bowls on stalks. (It's good to do this early as it's the chief place where you might encounter a queue.) Each bowl offers a different water massage: first right, for ankles, calves and thighs; first left for lower back - wonderful for sciatica and lumbago. The furthest pool has water jets of different intensities for a neck and shoulder massage.

Bowls finished with, swim across the lagoon and head outside down a flowing 'river' of warm water. (In winter steam rises all around you as your body keeps underwater and your head is out in the snowy cold.) Lie back on the underwater benches at the far end and gaze up at the surrounding mountain peaks whilst bubbles gently tone up your thighs.

Back inside try the Indo-Roman baths: 14°C and 36°C respectively. Frankly I skip the Indo part!

From there make your way to the back of the complex and, if feeling brave, paddle in the footbaths on the right, first standing in the warm water and then in the melt ice. Supposed to do wonders for the circulation.

Next comes a quick dash through a mist room and then on to the Turkish Hammam. The first time I went in I thought I'd suffocate in the steam but now I love it. Incredibly relaxing as well as cleansing. Saunas come next but I head on round the corner to the *Llum de Wood*. (*Llum* means light and here they use a type of Ultraviolet lighting invented by the American, R.W. Wood) This is a blissful relaxation room charged with energizing negative ions where you lie back, eyes closed to the muted, violet light and listen in silence to soothing sounds of pan pipes or waves breaking on the seashore.

There's a whole menu of massages too but it's best to book those in advance. If you like your pleasures child-free then why not visit the latest, upmarket installation, the Inúu, for personalized attention.

There's also a member's area where you can simply chill out: a bit of massage, dip into the newspapers, take a coffee with friends, then enjoy such exotica as a grapefruit pool where you rub your skin with the fruit bobbing around you! I noted a strong temptation to pick one up and throw it – but then remembered this was a Club!

Summer Festivals

As mentioned at the start of the book every town and even the tiniest hamlet has its *Festa Major*. Almost all happen during the summer and almost all the events are free. *Festes* can last from two to five days. Days filled with music and dance, pageantry, workshops, alfresco food and drink, competitions, children's entertainment and discos that can party on well into the small hours of the morning sometimes to the distress of the local canine population - and their owners.

Museums:

Ideal for the odd rainy day. Andorra has a plethora of small but interesting museums. Visit:

https://www.tripadvisor.co.za/Attractions-g190391-Activities-c49-Andorra.html

for a brief summary of most of them and do check out the reviews. If only given time for one, I would head for the Miniature Museum in Ordino and look at the extraordinary work of Nicolai Siadristy: his signature in gold on the cross-section of a hair; a woman standing alone on the shore watching a fishing boat heading out to sea, all sculpted on a grain of rice. The exhibits are quite simply breath-taking. A small museum with a big Wow! factor. The only other place in the world where they are on display is in Siadristy's home town of Kiev, Ukraine.

And then there's all the rest:

Horse riding and week-long pony trekking, climbing water falls and 17 different iron ways, swinging through the woods at treetop height or white water rafting and kayaking just across the border. Add to that all the two wheeled stuff including motor cross excursions.

To enhance your enjoyment, most tourist offices now carry an English language rundown of all the cultural events planned for the coming week plus a set of instructions on how to find them.

Also try the government web site:

http://visitandorra.com/en/

to learn more about what the country has to offer.

To ascend the slopes of Andorra
I use a nice comfy Land Rover
I could hike up the paths
But my legs wouldn't last
Soon I'd be pushing up daisies and clover.

DEATH IN CALDEA

FICTION

by Ursula Simpson Ure

High in the Pyrenees, the Caldea stencilled its pinnacle against the sky. A glittering tower buttressed by mirrored pyramids, reflecting the sun, the sky, the moon, the stars.

Inside the Caldea all was warm, clean and clear. Light was domed, music played. People swung round in Jacuzzi baths resembling giants' tea cups, or cannibals' super-modern cooking pots. Green, blue and crystalline Futuroscope.

In the Roman baths, the Turkish baths, the Finnish baths, clients were steamed to a delicate pink, refreshed with icy showers, or rolled on a bank of snow.

It had snowed a lot that Christmas. Up above the Tristaina lakes a few misguided isards tremblingly put tiny pointed hooves into the virgin snow. Most had fled. Hunters in jeeps with rifles and telescopic sights had decimated their wild and gentle herds. Small pellets of isard dung, not much bigger than rabbit droppings, fell in the snow, marking their wary and forlorn presence.

Lower down was the Balma de la Margineda where thousands of years ago prehistoric man had his dwellings and his burial grounds, beside a vast lake. No lake now. Banks guard the burial grounds, car parks and cosmetic houses line the fields of frescoes and dadoes imported from France and Spain.

The old people of the Balma de la Margineda, small people, who suffered from cancer and rheumatoid arthritis in the bones, lay silent, waiting perhaps for the long lost sound of lake water, for their riverine community to be re-born, drowning the glitzy, the tawdry, the pushy, 'go ahead' syndrome of modern Andorra. Little dark people sleeping unquietly.

In the Caldea the tourists were happy. Hot baths, thermal water, steaming ice. Massage, friction, thrills!

Lying back in the revolving Jacuzzi, pleasantly bubbled underneath and seduced above by lights and music and spouting fountains, Emma spun slowly, lapped in pleasure. Above her, diners in the restaurant looked down at the eerie white limbs in the emerald translucence of the thermal water. It was nearly half past nine on one of the holiday nights. It was not crowded but the animation was there, late comers and sybarites were enjoying this swinging, looming, splashing human aquarium.

The pool or lagoon in the main hall of the Caldea stretched outside, part within, part without. Outside the air was sharply cold and it had been snowing until now and steam rose up concealing the bathers, if there were any, from the snowy mountains and the swimmers indoors. All was shrouded, misty.

"It looks," Emma thought, poaching gently, "like a modernistic stage set for Swan Lake and the mere where those oddly named Willies were supposed to appear and lure strangers to their doom. Willies? Will-o'-the-Wisps?"

As she looked and the music surged and the fountains spouted, she thought for a moment that she discerned someone or something out there in the mist.

Oh, she had gone out there for a quick glimpse, when the snow was falling. It was ethereal and spine-chilling. Now the night was clear but the snow was close all around them. Bored with her futuristic cannibal pot, she stepped out. She was going to schlep to the Wet Foot Bar for 'un petit remontant'. Dry Martini? Champagne? Gin fizz? Side Car? Bloody Mary?

"Why not take all of them," she sang to the tune of 'Why not Take All of Me', humming softly, schlepping and schlopping towards the Bar.

Emma had very good long-distance sight and the movement she thought she saw in the outer lagoon, despite the mist, had for a moment transfixed her. Now, as she peered again, uneasy, she was sure of some violence, some evil in the mist. An amethyst colour, pale Burgundy, was spreading out against the background of the icy peaks and suddenly the fountains, drawing water from the outer pool spurted Burgundy, Bordeaux, Merlot. In the ice blue pools around her the water was turning lavender.

"How original," a cultured English voice spoke in her ear. "They are sending us home bathed in wine! What a pity it doesn't flow free and undiluted from the fountains."

At that moment, in the outer lagoon, the mist parted and Emma saw a sad, deflated, emptying human sack, half-submerged, bleeding what was left of his life into the pool. At the same time someone screamed; a high piercing wail of horror. The bar-tender stopped shaking the Maitai she had asked for. The stranger beside her put a firm hand on her arm.

"I see you don't scare easily. Good girl."

Emma said, "It's blood. A man's blood. We were both bathing in…."

The lights faltered, the music stopped.

"Ladies and Gentlemen! Please stay calm. There has been an accident. Please vacate the pools and swimming area immediately."

The Jacuzzis stopped. There was a growing murmur and a rush of thudding sliding feet. A woman in the restaurant stood up and pointed, screaming, until someone slapped her. The music came on again louder but the lights dimmed; people were hurrying in every direction, plunging like dolphins away from the spreading stain in the water towards the showers and changing rooms, dry land, normality. A woman cried as she fell, slipping on water-skiddy marble. Someone shouted in French for help.

Again a voice over the loud speaker called for calm. "There is no need to leave the restaurant, just evacuate the water area. Thank you."

Emma at the bar, was not willing to give up her Maitai, her luxury, her glorious Caldean evening. The bartender, eye rolling, responded to her gesture and filled the cocktail glass to the rim. She sucked in the alcohol and subtle additives. Delicious, she thought, absently - the final experience: snow, water, mist - and death.

Beside her the man said "I say that looks rather good - how coolly you sip it! My dear girl, this is the most extraordinary experience - I say Bar Man, another of these what-jeme-call-its, please!"

"Maitai," she said softly.

"Of course you may! Anything dear charmer, you name it!"

Emma looked at him, her eyes golden and lazy. "What a lovely old buffer," she thought, "and not so old either -."

"Please will you evacuate the pool area. There has been an accident. Please recover your clothes and wait until we give you permission to leave. Do not leave the premises for the moment."

"Who wants to?" Emma said.

"Quite right! Stick it out to the end! As for that poor bugger - couldn't be more sorry for him - still, there must be worse ways to go than looking at the mountains. Snow, lights, music, luxury. No, I reckon he's not too badly off. To die in a pool at midnight."

"It's only half nine."

"Well, whatever - What do you suppose? Mafia? Smuggling war? Vendetta? A long slim knife between the ribs when he was all relaxed and happy?"

They were clearing the area. The barman clicked his teeth and gracefully poured them the last sob from the shaker.

They picked their way through lavender water towards the locker rooms.

"An evening like this - what about going somewhere? Grilled prawns, sole, champagne? A little avocado salad?"

Emma lowered her eyes modestly. "It sounds delightful. But not here."

"Heavens no! Need to clear our thoughts."

"Were you in the war?" she asked him.

"So many wars! Not the bow and arrow ones of course, but, yes, wars: desert wars, jungle wars, nasty, never again! Snow wars, underwater wars, up in the sky wars. Yes a few."

When she joined him with her changing bag and her coat and her big shawl, he helped her carefully into the coat and took her bag and shawl from her. She didn't see him slip the long, fine-honed blade into the shawl. Even if she had she probably wouldn't have cared, nor been surprised. Tonight was not altogether real and from the moment he had touched her she had known that the adrenaline flowing in him and across to her, was incredible and electric. Who, after all, was the sad sagging sack of a man dying in the outer pool? Wasn't it enough that his blood had turned the world within the Caldea to a shocking pink?

There was an 'entrepreneur' from Valencia
Who applied here for his Residencia
When the Andorrans took a look
At the young man's bank book
He was rejected outright 'in absentia'.

ROMANTIC ROMANESQUE

and other pleasures

by J.P. Wood

Enter the village and parish churches of Andorra and enter a world of medieval showmanship.

Look and you will see paintings, frescos and murals, sufficient to imagine every inch of these walls covered in brilliant colour. See through the eyes of chiefly illiterate farmers and peasants whose hard daily grind is punctuated only by the ceremonies of Sundays and Feast Days, by the rites of baptisms, weddings and funerals. Inside the church they find an awe-inspiring world quick with life in the flickering candle and torchlight. Here, for the attentive congregation, are vivid pictures of their origins: the Creation; their obligations: the Commandments; their destinations: Heaven or Hell. Here too are thrilling scenes of martyrdoms and battles. It is the best of theatre.

The priest in his vestments, not as glorious as those of city clergy, but still bright compared to the drab of his congregation, stands with his back to them facing the East, facing blessed Jerusalem and the rising, life-giving sun - at least where the capricious mountains have permitted this orientation. The Latin is perhaps incomprehensible but the familiar intonations are soothing to the sweating or chilled families and neighbours who stand or kneel, shoulder to shoulder in momentary and possibly malodorous companionship. There is no heating or air-conditioning and outside is the stink of a medieval village. No matter. They are community, united in the hope of salvation, even if occasionally eyes stray to a bonny neighbour, or children fidget and pinch each other.

After Mass, the villagers will gather outside whatever the weather, discuss trade and exchange news and scandal. Perhaps the priest will have a word with those who need help, or chastisement. On feast days there will be food and drink, dancing. Young ones will flirt; old ones will plan matches and weddings and shake their heads at the ways of the young. Sometimes there is the slow, solemn procession to see a loved one or neighbour to his or her final resting place in a slot in the nearby cemetery wall. Burials are impossible in a terrain where even the churches have no foundations but rest upon solid rock.

Andorra, from the ninth century, had been part of the Diocese of Urgell. The Bishop's Episcopal See, La Seu d'Urgell, lies just over the border within Spain. Its splendid cathedral is **Santa Maria d'Urgell**, once known as the cathedral of Andorra. Consecrated in 837, its origins are pre-Romanesque. In the 11th century it was rebuilt and it is worth visiting for its Romanesque beauty which leans more towards the Italianate than the French, unsurprisingly since its primary architect was Raimondo Lombardi. Take a turn around its lovely tranquil cloisters. On three sides of the cloisters (alas the columns on the fourth side were sold off in 1603 at a time of extreme poverty) the exquisitely carved capitals show interestingly disagreeable fates for sinners, and rather more optimistic scenes for the virtuous. If you look closely, you will see that some of these have been numbered. This was in the 1920s in order to transport the cloister, stone by stone, to the United States for an

American millionaire who was under the illusion that he had purchased them. The deal fell through after a public outcry. The audio-visual presentation of the Beatus of La Seu, an illustrated, 10th Century Apocalypse, is fascinating for its insight into medieval morality and teaching.

From the 11th century, there was a flurry of church building throughout Europe. With Episcopal encouragement, the people of Andorra helped hew local stone to build their places of worship. None is large, after all the country itself is small, but some are very small indeed, scarcely larger than some of the shepherd and animal shelters dotting the mountain pastures. The church of **Les Bons** sitting above Encamp is no more than a nave, an apse and a very small porch. These porches, some added at a later date, are a common feature. If you have been in Andorra in deepest winter or the zenith of a summer's morning, you will understand why. For walkers, **Sant Cerni of Nagol**, a mini jewel of a place on the sunny slopes above Sant Julià, is well worth making the focus of a hiking excursion although it is perfectly easy to drive there.

What was common to all the churches was their place in the village or parish as centres of religion. The people who helped build these had a tremendous sense of ownership which would sadly prove to be false. Mid tenth century, the feudal princes of Andorra, the Comtes d'Urgell, gradually passed over their entitlement to the tithes and taxes of Andorra to the Bishopric. Agreements between the Andorrans and the Bishop in 1162 and 1176 saw the Bishop's powers encompass Church, Military, (all families had to provide one male to defend the causes of the bishop) and finally Justice.

As the ownership of village churches changed, so too did their role. Tithes and taxes, mostly in kind, were paid there. Proportions of the harvest went to the Bishop, proportions to the clergy. If you wished to impress you could pay some of the tithe in olive oil, the priest's portion serving for both culinary and ritual purposes, which is why you will find baptismal water fonts and baptismal oil fonts. The latter were not only used for welcoming infants into the body of the church but for the collection of the precious oil imported from way down in Spain.

When the role of the churches changed, so did the priestly role. Not only was the *Mossèn* (priest) now spiritual leader of his flock, he was a giver of news and announcements from outside the borders and first in the chain leading to earthly retribution

If, when you first set eyes on Andorran churches, you experience a strong sense of déjà-vu, don't rub your eyes or shake your head. The little guardian demons and angels have not transported you hundreds of kilometres (or weeks on horseback) to France or Italy. During the eleventh and twelfth centuries, construction was under the direction of travelling companies of Master Builders, stone masons and Master Painters. These were mostly natives of Lombardy, (although some were local, such as the Master of Santa Coloma and the Master of La Cortinada). They travelled throughout Western Europe, building in the Romanesque style, (or *Art Romànic* as they say in Catalan) with Byzantine elements brought back by the Crusaders; a case of early pan-Europeanism?

These busy craftsmen built and painted virtually from pattern books, at huge speed and with very little opportunity for individuality. In **the Romanesque Audio-visual centre in Pal**, you can find two rather lovely models of the most common pattern of Romanesque church, **Santa Eulalia of Encamp** with a soaring bell tower (at twenty-three metres, one of the tallest in Andorra) a semi-circular apse and porch and **Sant Cerni of Nagol** with a more solid campanile tower, semi-circular apse and porch,.

Not all churches adhere strictly to this pattern. The church of **Sant Cristòfol** of Anyós is distinctly maverick, with a small square capped bell tower and a bell whose dull tones are minatory.

Santa Coloma, one of Andorra's most glorious churches in the village of that name, has a round tower unique in Andorra and rare in the Pyrenees. It is pre-Romanesque in origin and was decorated with 12th century Romanesque mural paintings by the Master of Santa Coloma. These paintings left the country in 1930 and were recovered by the Andorran government in 2007.

Nearby, strategically positioned on a hill above Santa Coloma, is the little church of **Sant Vicenç** an intriguing example of what was a fortified complex. The church was restored in the 1970's and is well worth walking to but beware cold winter mornings. The rocky path to the church can be filmed with ice and treacherous to all but the young and very agile. Wait until the sun hits the mountain.

In the **Romanesque Audio-visual centre**, you can find a facsimile of one of the few remaining pattern books for frescos with the formula for the characteristic figures of the time. Walls were plastered with wet pigment which helped fill in irregularities; forms and figures were pricked out in red pigment, even going as far as to indicate the accepted level of the eyes with a straight red line. The paintings were then completed and touched up in dry pigment.

Despite this pattern-book building and painting, the walls and towers of these churches are lent individuality by the local materials - different slates, limestone, pumice (because of its vegetable lightness useful for curved arches and carved elements) and, where it is available, granite. If your first impression is of grey, you are mistaken. Within these stones are violet, amber, rose and dove tints to make a Parisian designer drool.

Magnificent, bully-boy gothic, which so changed the form of ecclesiastical and civic building in Western Europe, had little effect in Andorra. When you go to the **Romanesque Audio-visual centre** in Pal, one of the best-preserved villages in the country, take a guided tour of **Sant Climent** of Pal. There you can see a few traces of the Gothic, more naturalistic figures flexing a little to left or right and the remains of wall paintings which are purely ornamental, an escape from the Romanesque norm filling every church wall with rigid and iconic figures broadcasting moral messages.

After viewing the church take a walk around the steep streets of the village, the stone walls brightened by vivid gardens. On the main road you can see the *safareig* or wash-place where in the old days women used to exchange news while scrubbing their clothes in water which can only have been glacial. *Safareig* became a term for gossip; today a column of one of the local newspapers, *Set Dies*, bears that name.

Poverty, isolation, artistic inertia and perhaps a preference for what is, maintained the status quo for centuries. The next surge of building was in the late 16th century baroque period with its nostalgia for the past. Areas of Andorra had grown more prosperous in iron mining or wool. The local grandees wished to prove their wealth and devotion and those churches nearest to the sources of wealth benefited. Towers were raised, floors were lowered or raised and doors were moved. All of which permitted the installation of larger artefacts. Some rather nice baroque altarpieces date from this era.

Traditionally the reredos at the back of the altar is topped by God the Father. Saint John the Baptist holds his lamb, and the Gospel. The Immaculate Conception shows the Virgin crowned with a sunburst and striding the crescent moon. Saint Paul is there with his sword, Saint Peter clutches outsized keys. There is always an image of the Virgin in one or other of her roles. Our Lady of Remedies was particularly popular in an isolated country dependent on herbs and simples to cure their ills and frequently in need of a little divine backing. The Patron Saint or Saints of the church figure too, holding their emblems of sanctity and martyrdom. Below them are often dramatic little carved scenes of torture and saintly exploits.

As the mining of iron spread, around altars and side chapels appeared traces of this new wealth, fine iron gates donated by the wealthy. You can imagine the donors sitting there of a Sunday beguiled from the sermon by the value and beauty of their contributions.

The next building boom for the churches in the twentieth century would be more of restoration and the uncovering of long hidden paintings, the retrieval of lost artefacts. However, if you think that the Romanesque style vanished, you are mistaken. **Sant Cerni de Canillo** was built in the 18th century and shows very few deviations from the Romanesque form. The ruins of tiny **Sant Andreu,** in one of the elegant suburbs of Andorra La Vella, were completely reconstructed in perfect Romanesque style, leaving the church looking older than the stately oaks surrounding it. Inside, are paintings by a well-loved twentieth century Andorran artist, Carmen Mas, showing her family and neighbours who helped refurbish the church. **Sant Pere Màrtir** in Escaldes, built in 1956 by Josep Danés in honour of the wool dressers and weavers, is pure neo-Romanesque. The church contains the works of contemporary Andorran artists, Sergi Mas and Josep Viladomat.

Most notable, is the church/minor Basilica of **Nostra Senyora de Meritxell**, patron saint of Andorra. Designed by the architect, Ricard Bofill, in 1974 to replace the original church burnt down in 1972, (accident or arson, the jury is out), the design is elegantly modern but the external constructions still echo the Romanesque.

If you visit the churches of Andorra during the summer months, you will not be bored. The guides are excellent and knowledgeable and there is scarcely a church without a view to die for. However, like me, you may come away remembering more of the quirky, the different, the odd.

From the **Cathedral of La Seu**, you may remember the Beatus because in 1996, a French schoolteacher and his partner, with the use of tear gas, stole the book. It disappeared, seemingly forever, but was recovered ten years later when his disgruntled ex-partner shopped him to the police. Two pages were missing from the document and never recovered. You may also remember the crowds gathered around the main gate staring up at a monkey thoroughly misbehaving himself. The savage winged beasts on either side of him are a grim warning against the sin of onanism, but like so many minatory ecclesiastical works throughout the ages, more of a draw than a deterrent.

In **Sant Cristòfol**, Anyós, my favourite, my local church, there's a 16th century mural showing Saint Christopher carrying the Christ-child across the river. This bears no resemblance to the austere Romanesque figures. The giant looks bewildered by the weight of the tiny figure on his shoulders; through transparent water, small fish nibble at his feet. In the background are two versions of the church itself plus, unsurprisingly, mountains and, more astonishingly, a glimpse of the sea and ships. The oil font still maintains its wooden lid. (In other churches these fonts can only be differentiated by a small protuberance on the stone rim which acted as a hinge to the long rotted cover.) If you are here on 10th July, Saint Christopher's Day, come up and have your car blessed. You may have to queue a bit with police cars, fire vehicles, garbage trucks and the odd pony or bike.

Sant Martí de La Cortinada sits in the pretty village of that name and is particularly memorable for a seventeenth century carillon, a musical instrument that imitates the peals of bells.

On 15th August, crowds make the pilgrimage up to lovely **Canolich**, isolated in the hills above Sant Julià. They attend Mass and afterwards, the priest hands out blessed bread to the picnicking multitudes. It is a delightful walk but you can drive there if the ascent makes you feel a little faint-hearted.

Another place of pilgrimage is the **Sanctuary of Nostra Senyora de Meritxell** on the 8th of September, the national day of Andorra. Crowds, thousands strong, young and old, go on foot from all parts of the country to honour the nation's patroness. This sanctuary is also a place where couples go on the third Sunday in June to re-pledge their wedding vows. If you feel ultra-energetic, on the third Sunday of August, there's a race to **Santa Coloma** to celebrate that church's feast day.

Sant Joan de Caselles, at the side of the main road in the parish of Canillo, is a handsome, solid church, the nave particularly notable for a framework of wood and the ghost of a once splendid Christ in Majesty including a wooden bas relief of Christ's head, some rather better preserved murals and stuccos, and a necropolis indicating that once there was a settlement nearby. Your abiding memory nowadays may be of a filigree crowd of cows, relicts of the recent glorious LandArt exhibition, set to become a biennial event in Andorra. (The cows have now gone.)

If you want a pleasant day out, try **Sant Miquel** of Engolasters. Built in the 12th Century, it has a long, elegant bell tower (17 metres) with double arch windows without partitions. The tower is disproportionate to the absurdly small nave huddled at its side, possibly to give a view of the fields and buildings on the surrounding plateau which cannot have changed much over the last centuries. Afterwards, walk around the legendary lake of Engolasters or walk up the Madriu valley, declared a World Heritage site by UNESCO in 2004. After that, I would recommend a long lunch in one of the restaurants overlooking the lake

There are so many things to see, not all ecclesiastical. If you go to Les Bons above Encamp to see the church of **Sant Romà**, visit the historical complex, mostly ruined, made up of the **Castle of Les Bons** and the **Moors' tower.** Also go to **Sant Romà de Vila** on the other side of Encamp.

Sant Esteve, the parish church of Andorra La Vella, incorporates the remains of a Romanesque temple although throughout the ages, the church has been restored and added to. The last additions were by the contemporary architect Josep Puig i Caldfach who remodelled the bell tower and the lateral entrance which we see today. Inside are two baroque altar pieces, one from the 17th century dedicated to Saint Lucy (whose fair in Andorra la Vella is a considerable Christmas attraction) and one from the 18th century, dedicated to Saint John the Baptist. Just beyond the church, up a narrow cobbled street to the old town lies the handsome **Casa de la Vall**, ancient seat of government, place of judgement on ill-doers, witches and the place where the last death sentence on a fratricide was decreed on 18th October, 1945.

Go in the other direction out into the main town and all the pleasures of a modern shopping metropolis are yours for the taking.

In July and August there are coach tours to the principal churches.

(See: www.visitandorra.com)

Many of the smaller churches are manned or womanned by students. At your approach there will be a flutter of closing pages as they toss the latest best-seller aside. Last year 'Shades of Grey' hit the dust, next year who knows. They will leap to their feet, eager to practise their English and tell you all about their local church.

Exhausted? Go and stand on one of the Romanic bridges and feel the clean spray of mountain streams against your skin. The **La Margineda** bridge between Sant Julià de Lòria and Santa Coloma allows you to cross the river Valira, whilst the **Sant Antoni** bridge (once the only way to approach La Massana), down in the gorge between the tunnels leading northwards towards the town, gives you a sinister view of the chapel of **Sant Antoni de la Grella**. Stand still long enough and, against the roar of the foaming water, you may hear the susurrus of leather soles, the clop of mule and horses. In the case of **Sant Antoni**, you may also hear the roar of the devil riders reputed to have nearly terrified the life out of a drunken young man returning late to see his sweetheart. It is said that he built the chapel in gratitude to the saint for saving him from the demonic horde. His name was Ton (Antoni).

Jaded now? Hungry? La Massana lies up the road offering a cornucopia of bars and restaurants.

This is a guide to the churches of Andorra and not a restaurant guide, but sight-seeing is hungry work, and eating is part of the traveller's pleasure. A glass of wine will probably not come amiss either.

Enjoy.

Engolasters Church is quite small,
But its tower is incredibly tall
For something that old
(Four hundred years, I've been told)
It's a wonder the thing doesn't fall.

8 FESTIVAL

8th September Meritxell Day & Andorra's National Day.

First, a word of warning. EVERYTHING is closed in Andorra for Meritxell Day. Despite the introduction, in 1993, of Constitution Day (March 14th), Meritxell remains the most important, and solemn, of the country's national celebrations.

As with many traditions in Andorra, this one dates back to the Middle Ages - a time of great upheaval all along the northern slopes of the Pyrenees. Christianity and Paganism were fighting for the hearts and minds of the people. Similar legends to that of Our Lady of Meritxell can be found throughout the Pyrenees. A visit to the Cathedral Museum in La Seu will reveal at least eight 'miraculous' Madonnas dating from the same period. The original 12th century statue of the Madonna and Child from Canòlich (surrounded by a comparable legend) can be found in the church of Sant Julià de Lòria.

The Legend of Our Lady of Meritxell

It was Three Kings, Epiphany, 6th of January, and very cold. Some people coming up from the direction of Encamp were taking the snow-covered path to Canillo to hear Mass when, to their astonishment, they saw a dog-rose, green-leafed and in full bloom. They went closer to see what sort of marvel this was and there, under the bush, they found a brightly painted wooden statue of the Virgin and Child. They picked her up and carried her to the priest in Canillo. He put her on the altar and, after Mass, locked the church and went home to bed. The following morning he unlocked the church. And lo! The statue had disappeared.

On taking the path home the pilgrims found to their astonishment that the statue had returned to the foot of the dog-rose. Could it perhaps be that she would prefer to be in Encamp rather than Canillo? They picked her up and carried her carefully down the path to Encamp, handed her to the priest who put her on the altar, locked the door and went home to bed. The next day he unlocked the church and found the statue had disappeared. So the people returned to Meritxell and, lo and behold, they found her yet again under the bush. They then realised that that was where she wanted them to build a sanctuary.

* * * *

After that, the tiny hamlet of Meritxell, first documented in 1176, became a centre of pilgrimage for the whole of the medieval Pyrenees just as modern day pilgrims converge on Lourdes. There is a fascinating ledger which was kept by the priests, noting down all the gifts given to the Sanctuary including such things as wax candles and a bell rope. Over the centuries, thanks in part to the pilgrims, Canillo became the most prosperous parish in Andorra.

After a request from the Consell General (Andorra's parliament) in 1913, Pope Pius X gave permission for Our Lady of Meritxell to be declared the Patroness of Andorra. The 8th September was declared a national holiday and the Sanctuary became a symbol of Andorran nationality. For some 50 years (before the Constitution of 1993 separated church and state), the Síndic, (chairman of the Consell

General), gave the State of the Nation address outside the Sanctuary after Mass. He would record the events of the past year and tell of the Council's plans for the next.

On 8th September, 1972, during the night following the Meritxell celebrations, the old sanctuary mysteriously burnt down. At first it was thought to be an accident and that the 12th century statue had been destroyed. But then it was realised that among the ashes there was no sign of the precious stones that studded her gold crown. It appeared that the statue had been stolen, never to be found, and the fire was an act of arson.

Today the ancient chapel has been simply restored to serve as a museum to the new, imposing Sanctuary of Meritxell, a little forbidding from the outside but bathed in light and superb views from within.

AUTUMN

(and back to Winter)

So many trees fell
last winter. Their shards
set our stove ablaze.

Valerie Rymarenko

5

The Countryside: Then and Now

by Clare Allcard

Long, long ago during the time of Andorra's Arcadian idyll, it is said that every Andorran family had a plot of land, a *borda* (small stone farmhouse), a farmyard and a kitchen garden. They grew enough cereals and vegetables and raised enough livestock to feed themselves. Vines for wine grew on the lower, south-facing slopes. They hunted and fished. They gathered nuts. They probably grew hemp and flax for textiles. They even had their own communal assembly. By the 9th century a number of today's villages were already established.

For the next thousand years the people followed nature's rhythm though each parish had its own traditions. For instance in the past century or two, Sant Julià specialised in goats. Each morning the village goatherd would go round the houses collecting the goats and then drive the flock up into the hills to graze. It was these goats that provided Andorra's babies with milk if their mothers were unable to breastfeed.

The agricultural year was dictated by different designated Saints days in the different parishes. (There is as much as a month between the advent of spring in relatively low lying Sant Julià and its arrival in the higher parishes.) Thus in Canillo it was Easter Monday when a child as young as six or seven might be chosen to go up with some livestock into the mountains. If he or she was lucky, a dog would go too for company. Once a week someone would bring the child food: bread and sausage, cheese and potatoes and perhaps a bowl of nourishing soup. Sounds pretty harsh to our ears but wait a moment: quite possibly the child was proud to be thought old enough for such family responsibility. Indeed a friend's uncle told her that, as a child, he had envied his older brother when, aged seven or eight, he was allowed to take the sheep up into the mountains whilst he, two years younger, had to stay in the village and mind the cows.

As the sun rose ever higher in the sky, Canillo's villagers would leave their stone houses in the valleys *en masse* and drive their main flocks and herds, often from the animals' winter home in France, to the high summer pastures or *cortals* (a word still found in place names today), there to fatten them up on lush grass and copious wild flowers. On Sundays a few of the men would return to the valley to make sure all was well in the village and, once a month, an itinerant priest would visit the different *cortals* to say Mass in their miniscule chapels.

Take one of the many marked walking trails into Canillo's high pastures today and there you may stumble across the ruins of a cluster of dry-stone-walled *bordes*. Sit a while and look around you. Drink in the silence and the beauty of the mountains. For this is where the villagers spent their summers. Imagine a small boy sitting on that very same hillside overseeing the family's sheep while his father tended to the larger beasts and any sick animals or else toiled in the sun tilling the earth. For here, on the high, sunny, or *solà,* side of the valleys, part of the land was sown with rye and the vegetable patch with peas and beans. Chickens clucked and cocks crowed and the family's pigs rootled in the earth. Women and girls milked the sheep and cows and boiled up ewe's milk to make cheese. Sadly, today Andorra's air is almost totally devoid of that penetrating sound of cock-crow so warmly resonant of our collective past. Indeed even tractors are now becoming rarer.

The *obac,* or shady side of the valleys, was left forested, husbanded by the comuns; woodcutting was, and still is, strictly regulated. Firewood could only be gathered from fallen branches or dead trees. Anyone wishing to fell live trees for building had to submit a request and anyone wanting trees from an avalanche zone had to apply to the Verguers, the personal representatives of the co-princes themselves. Even then they could only cut down one tree in three. Despite this, where today the hillsides around Ordino are thickly forested, 60 years ago there was only open grassland where the cattle grazed.

Between the 16th and the beginning of the 20th century Andorra's greatest source of income was livestock; Canillo's extensive highlands attracted herds from far afield. Known as the Transhumance, huge flocks travelled on hoof as much as 250 miles from the Camargue in France and from Extremadura in Spain. As early as 1264 mention is made of a bridge being built to carry the cattle of the Transhumance across Andorra's main, Gran Valira, river. The year 1909 alone saw 30,000 sheep, 200 cattle, 300 mules and 100 horses travel from Spain's steaming summer plains to Andorra's refreshing uplands.

With such huge flocks the shepherds had to be well organised. Theirs was big business. An overseer, several ordinary shepherds and often a shepherd boy took charge of the sheep on their long trek ever upwards. The overseer appointed one of the shepherds as *mestressa.* His job, as the name suggests, was to cook, mend clothes and cater for the others. Often a mule accompanied the team to transport water, cooking pots and food.

Horses, cows and oxen were fitted with different types of bell according to kind: the horses' bell was made of brass; the cows' of copper while the oxens', though also made of copper, was semi-spherical with its own distinctive ring. Thus, even in the dark, the herdsmen could tell by the sound which type of animal was straying.

Once the Transhumance arrived in Andorra the grazing sequence was carefully ordained. First all the animals had to spend time foraging in the valleys, helping to manure and enrich the fields. Then between Sant Bernabé and Sant Joan (11th and 24th June) the animals would gradually move up to the higher ground. The horses were first to be driven up to crop the tallest pastures preparing them for the cattle that could not cope with the longest grasses. Finally the sheep followed, nibbling what grass was left almost to the bare earth.

Here the migrant shepherds lived in rough, dry-stone huts, the ruins of which can still be found. Here, too, were the dry-stone sheepfolds or *pletes* (*La Pleta* is a favourite name for some of Andorra's fancier housing estates.) At night the shepherds wrapped themselves in sheepskins against the mountain chill. They had no furniture. A stone bench served as a bed. They drank and ate out of simple, hand-carved wooden bowls. Indeed the shepherds were famous for their carving, known as *musicat.* Around Sant Miquel, (29th September), they would once more start their descent.

The highlight of the pastoral season was undoubtedly Andorra la Vella's Fair. Dating back into antiquity, it was first recorded as being held on October 27th in 1402, and an animal fair continues to be held on that same date to this day. For Andorra's parishes it signalled the end of the agricultural year.

Imagine it. The town seethes as people arrive from all over the country and beyond. Out in the designated pasture there's the constant bleat of sheep; the occasional lowing of cattle or neighing and stamping of horses. The smell of warm dung fills the air, while the gooseherd leads his honking flock to market. Hawkers' cries echo up and down the unpaved lanes of the town, offering everything from sewing thread to farm implements. They are also doing a brisk trade in homemade cakes, *allioli* (in those days a compound of garlic and oil) and *torró,* a type of nougat made with honey and almonds, an essential part of today's winter celebrations too.

This is also the time when stock is sold off, shepherds receive their wages and cattle owners look for winter homes for their larger beasts. Now, too, parish and church dues have to be paid; the latter based on livestock holdings.

But look, in the distance over there, do you catch a glimpse of the women from across the Spanish border riding their mules up the narrow track with panniers of fruit and vegetables swaying on either side? And from Santa Coloma, see the baskets filled to overflowing with chestnuts and walnuts! Everyone has come to sell their surpluses and, in exchange, to stock up with the staples: wine, sugar, oil and salt, needed to see them through the winter.

In 2013, the Andorra la Vella Trade Fair, held on the weekend nearest to 27th October and the ancient fair's direct descendent, lasted three days, covered some 11,000sq m in the centre of the capital, welcomed up to 150 exhibitors both from Andorra and across her borders. They offered a huge diversity of products ranging from cars and industrial equipment, furniture and double glazing through to local cheeses, wines, mint infusions and traditional pine cone medicines for the treatment of coughs, to hand-tooled leather goods, IT equipment and discounted ski passes. And, as in 1402, on 27th October itself, there was a livestock show, this time in the big international coach park in front of the government building.

Andorra remained self-sufficient in the by-products of stock-raising right up to the beginning of the 20th century. Originally wheat was grown in fertile fields by the rivers while the high grasslands were harvested for winter fodder for the animals. Viable fields for cereals however were always scarce in these rugged mountains, which is why, today, you can still see hill terracing where farmers and *comuns* banded together to create irrigation systems which in turn increased the arable land for cereals.

It was during the 17th century that tobacco began to appear along Andorra's riversides, grown for local consumption and for smuggling through the mountains and across the border to Spain where tobacco products were heavily taxed. Then, one day, Spain imposed the death penalty on anyone caught smuggling or selling tobacco within their borders which had not been grown there. Sort of put people off for a while.

Eventually the death penalty was lifted and the plant swept Andorra. In 1893 a visitor wrote, "Along the length of the river from Escaldes to Sant Julià you see innumerable plantations. At first sight you think it is allotments but then you realise the colour of the plants is purer than summer greens." It was tobacco.

But, alas, not of the highest quality. Another visitor reported that Andorran tobacco, "gave off a pestilential and insufferable stink so that one had to stand several metres away to avoid the acrid fumes!" In the early 20th century, in an effort to improve the quality, it became illegal to cultivate this smelly species of plant, though the local tobacco even today is of a rougher type, very high in nicotine, known as 'dark' tobacco.

Tobacco became the most profitable cash crop and all but ousted cereals from the fertile valley floors thus destroying the country's self-sufficiency in food. By the middle of the 20th century the country had become a monoculture. Tobacco was king.

Much of the crop was cultivated in small fields, so local cigarette manufacturers, mainly from Sant Julià and Andorra la Vella, would tour the villages collecting the 'packets' of pressed leaves for processing. The factory workers then turned the dark tobacco into cigars, cigarettes, pipe tobacco, chewing tobacco or snuff.

Today, the Reig Tobacco factory in Sant Julià has been transformed into an excellent Tobacco Museum – with a whole floor devoted to smuggling!

It wasn't until after World War Two that a great revolution took place in an Andorran industry that had remained pretty much unchanged over the last three hundred years. The United States entered the European cigarette market. Their lighter brands of tobacco flooded the shops. Europeans switched preferences in droves. A few European factories signed contracts with famous US brands. This meant that, just as McDonald's franchises have to source their meat from specified vendors, so the European franchised factories had to source their raw tobacco from the United States from where it arrives today in great, plastic-wrapped bales. As French and Spanish smokers switched allegiance, local Andorran farmers suffered.

So a delegation took their worries to the Permanent Delegate of the French Co-prince in Perpignan and petitioned his help. And the Permanent Delegate listened. And acted. His position was simple. Raw US tobacco was reaching American-affiliated Andorran factories via France. For that to continue, the cigarette companies would have to include at least some Andorran tobacco in their finished product. (The Episcopal Co-Prince in Spain also lent his support.)

In 1974, a contract was signed in Perpignan and a Tobacco Association formed between international manufacturers and Andorran farmers. The basis of that agreement holds good to this day.

When it comes to the actual cultivation of tobacco, each parish, depending on its altitude, has a different timetable for planting and harvesting.

In Ordino, for instance, it was traditionally on the first Friday of March that farmers or their wives sprinkled the tobacco seeds into seed trays. At the end of May the family transplanted the seedlings in neat rows into the fields. All they then needed was water, sunshine and the odd weeding. In times gone by, when summer hailstorms threatened, the church bells would ring out in a frantic effort to break up the clouds. Thirty years ago farmers still fired rockets into the air to ward off hail; it needs only one brief hailstorm to shred handsome, full-grown tobacco leaves to pathetic, useless tatters. Around Sant Corneli, 16th September, the flowers on each plant had to be topped or removed by hand before Ordino's tobacco harvest could begin.

Once harvested, the leaves were, and still are, hung up to dry. In the old days it was a common sight to see garlands of long, wrinkling tobacco leaves strung on string tied to nails on cottage walls or hanging high up in barns. Today you see the leaves hung to dry in ventilated sheds or the attics of old bordes.

Later, while the tobacco is still a little damp and flexible, the work of cutting it away from the central membrane begins. These pieces of leaf are then folded, made into a packet, and placed in a press.

During the year the Tobacco Association meets once or twice to discuss prices and quality. Once the tobacco is ready for sale, it is transported in 35-40kg bales to a large warehouse in Santa Coloma. On the appointed day, the farmers' commissioner and the buyers' commissioner meet there, with an Andorran government agriculture inspector also present. He oversees the buying and selling and keeps records of all the transactions, quantities and prices.

The buyers select what they want of the dark tobacco and ship it to France where, these days, it usually constitutes about 20% of the blended chewing tobacco for the American market.

From the time that tobacco took over the fertile fields, anyone who had the smallest plot of land would cultivate an *hort* or vegetable plot. With no refrigerators, even as recently as the 1950s, cabbage, potatoes and onions formed the unvarying winter diet for the vast majority of the people, with a daily serving of pork for protein. Presumably it was this that dictated the very popular dish *trinxat*: a hearty meal similar to British bubble and squeak made with chopped cabbage and potato and sometimes a little bacon. Most people had chickens and rabbits and they shot squirrels for squirrel soup said to make a very white broth. Lamb and chicken were for high days and holidays. Only those with flocks could eat lamb or mutton on a regular basis. There was no fish unless caught in the rivers or lakes. For this they either used their hands or a trident, three-pronged spear. No one had enough space in their small bordes to stable flocks of sheep over the winter so, with special dispensation from the Co-Princes, they were driven, tax-free, down to France as was the larger livestock, with a few cows kept back to provide milk. These, along with one or two pigs and some poultry, were kept on the ground floor of the houses so that, during the hard alpine winters, the heat from animals bodies helped to warm the folk living above.

In the summer people grew leeks and carrots, greens and lettuce, potatoes and cabbages plus a little wheat, though fancy foods like cauliflower or the delicate tomato were seldom seen. Any surplus would be used for barter. Someone offered to fix a window in their neighbour's house, and instead of cash in exchange, he'd receive a sack of potatoes or wool ready-spun for warm winter clothing.

At harvest time in the 1950's a threshing machine would arrive from la Seu, just across the border in Spain. It went from village to village threshing the families' few sheaves of wheat. Virtually every day the same town sent a Milk Co-op truck to collect all the spare milk to be taken across the border and processed.

It was not till the second half of the 20th century that farmers began to desert the land in droves for the more lucrative fields of commerce and tourism. The influx of migrants caused land prices to soar. Farmers sold off their tobacco fields - 'growing houses' was proving much more profitable. Between 1970 and 1990 the country's built-up area tripled. In forty years its population increased tenfold and its annual tourist 'crop' mushroomed from 300,000 to 10 million visits a year. Tourism and trade in goods and services had taken over from the traditional trade in livestock. In 1972 agriculture was 8.3% of the country's economy; by 2002 it was a mere 0.35%. In 2003 only 1,873 hectares was being farmed, 34% of that in the parish of Sant Julià. Of a total of 337 farms only 123 dealt in livestock. The total tobacco harvest was 326,552 kg whilst the value of imported tobacco was over 36 million euros.

Today, to halt the critical decline in the country's agricultural heritage and to add picturesque 'tourist appeal' to the summer slopes, the government offers livestock farmers generous subsidies for insurance, veterinary bills and stock improvement. This has lead to an increase in the number of Andorra's organically reared cattle, all of which receive a special stamp of *Carn de qualitat* which can be found in specialised shops in Andorra. The number of horses reared for meat has, from a very low base, actually doubled. What fields remain are still nearly all devoted to tobacco though, in recent years, locally prized potatoes – *trumfes* - and grapes for wine, quite common in medieval times, have also made a reappearance.

But even now the old ways can still return to enchant. A few years ago a friend and I packed a picnic and drove up past Pal and the Coll de la Botella to a rough trail on the border with Spain. We had just taken out our sandwiches when we heard the rarest of sounds: sheep bleating. We scanned the mountain slopes and the narrow pass ahead but to no avail and then, quite suddenly, they appeared. Hundreds upon hundreds of them undulating over a crest to the south then spreading out, an avalanche of white wool, to engulf the pastureland. Sharp on their heels and circling their peripheries ran a trio of sheepdogs deftly controlling the flock. Finally, from behind, came a lone shepherd. He brought with him the haunting sound of his reed pipe calling out through the pure mountain air. Once his flock had settled, he perched on a rock and continued to play. Bewitched, we sat in silence and soaked up the scene. In moments he had transported us back one thousand years to Andorra's Arcadian idyll.

A not-so-young lady from Llorts
Affected some very snug shorts
One day she bent over
To gather some clover
And that was the end of those shorts

NIGHT RIDE ON A BROOMSTICK

A gothic tale

by J. P. Wood

Alicia lies, arms and legs rigid beneath the covers. The footsteps of the night attendant fade down the corridor, accompanied by doors opening and closing with a *that's you sorted for the night, and no disturbance please* sort of clack. She hears the soft whirr and thump, pause, thump and whirr of the lift.

Tonight, pretty, plump Mireia is on duty. She will go to the office, glue herself to her mobile, cooing her way through a list of girlfriends, ending with a call in the small hours to titillate her latest beau with saucy promises she has no intention of keeping. There will be no disturbance from Mireia – Alicia knows because she has often eavesdropped on the girl, enjoying her naïve belief in herself as a femme fatale. When she wearies of prattling, the young woman will fall asleep over a copy of *Hola*, and wake and stretch at precisely fifteen minutes before the morning arrival of matron; just time enough to finish her report on a trouble-free night.

Other attendants like a little chat with the residents; they feel that this is just what the old dears need, rather than a sleeping tablet at nine o'clock sharp.

Which is why Alicia has chosen tonight; that and because the moon is full, a hunting moon, hanging in the October sky, low enough still to be pierced by the cone of Andorra's Pic Negre beyond the busy main road and dull buildings,

221

Mireia had wanted to draw the curtains, so Alicia whinged on about her claustrophobia until the girl pursed her face into a child's impression of disapproving authority.

'Very well!' Cross swish of fabric pushed back again. 'But don't let me hear you grumble about not sleeping,'

Not a bad girl, but silly, thinks Alicia, recalling the half-turned young face smoothed by moonlight to real beauty, murmuring. 'It is so romantic.'

Romantic! Such belittling poppycock!

Still, she would have liked to have brewed her a love potion as a farewell gift; to have thought of her queening it over others for a while.

'Excuse her, my Lady,' mutters Alicia to the moon almost filling the space between the wings of cute, animal-scattered cotton that someone thought appropriate to lift the hearts of the aged. 'She's very young.'

For a while, Alicia waits for sleep to fall on the Home, but not tranquillity. Oh no! The residents, released by their half-drugged sleep to relive old tenderness, old hates and old longings, moan and sigh and call out names. Besides which, they fart, cough and splutter, phlegm roiling around in chests weakened by the first winter agues.

Alicia, cursed with preternatural hearing, has listened to these sounds for thirteen months.

'It is time,' she says to the watching moon. The moon makes a sudden leap above the mountains and seems to bow towards her in dignified agreement.

Alicia kicks back the duvet, and rises, a little stiffly, but she's pretty good for someone a century old. She bows back to the moon. She goes to the capacious wardrobe and, from the very back recesses, fishes out a stick as thick as her wrist, which is not so very thick; then a bag, black with the scarlet emblem of the Pyrenees department store. The contents poke oddly against the shiny plastic, stretching the **P** into a serpent shape. From it, she extracts a squat, dimpled jar which appears empty of anything save a little dust.

The stick, held up against the window, bars the moon, like a warrior's spear. The wood is age-darkened, time-smoothed, and as she once explained to a surprised matron, very, very old; her Àvia's; which is why she wanted to keep it, and to further questions – yes her Àvia was a very tall woman. Whereupon Matron had stridden off down the corridor leaving Angels to help her unpack, muttering, 'Poor old bat, thinks a broom handle is her grandmother's walking stick – must have been a giantess then.'

Alicia strokes the stick and thinks that yes, her grandmother had been a giantess, capable of scaring tittle-tattling villagers, even into fits.

From the bag, she now draws out willow twigs as fine as lace. She tries to arrange them around the base of the stick but her hands are clumsy. She pauses, pokes crooked fingers into the jar, straining for the bottom where, after all, there seems to be a residue of something viscous. Whatever it is, she smooths it onto her hands, grimacing at its pungency, and dumps the jar on the table by the window which serves as desk, dining-table and dressing-table for whatever beautifying the old deem necessary – no mirror though.

Suddenly deft as a young woman, she places the stick next to the jar, gathers all the twigs together and knots them into place with her knee-highs, thinking how useful the flexible modern fabric is compared to the wilful split withy which, in the past, had so often scratched her fingers and broken her nails.

She lets her sensible nightdress pool around her feet. Standing in the light of the unconcerned moon, she scrapes around again in the jar. 'Belladonna, Mandragora, Bethany,' she warbles like a litany, and finally, 'fat,' but she does not specify what fat. Instead she rubs the stuff into her face and arms, and then a last scrape for her legs, a slick to her sparse pubic hair.

It is not a beauty product; that is for sure. Alicia's silvered body is still diminished and feeble, her breasts pockets voided of the beauty that once made men covet her: the white hairs on her head are as sparse against her knobbed skull as those at the vee of her groin. Her face, scored by those hundred years, is ugly, no other word for it. Still, her eyes in their walnut hammocks are brilliant, and she stands as straight against the white moon as the besom broom she now holds in her hands. 'Strength to the Lord,' she recites, caressing the handle, then whispers as she runs her fingers against the splayed twigs. 'Glory to the Lady.'

'Time,' she repeats, and she must have unlatched the broad windows, for they swing open onto the mountains crisp under the first snows, above them the sky clear and brittle as a glass dome.

Then Alicia is gone.

Somewhere, nearby, a dog howls up its wolfish ancestry and a cat shrieks a demonic counterpoint.

It is cold as Alicia soars over the well-trained trees and bushes in the dim gardens of the Home, although not as bitterly cold as when last she flew beneath the wolf moon, or snow moon. The air burns her throat, her eyes bulge a little, and water, but she does not care. The night and the circling mountains are hers. She is tugged towards the moon with a drunkard's craving for its harsh beauty, but her grandmother's words ring in her ears. 'Approach not the Mistress, Alicia. Wait until she calls you.' The old bat had a tendency to the theatrical but normally she got things right. Hadn't she leapt from the top of the walls of the old town on a day of the full Wolf Moon and been found at its base, arms outstretched as if in greeting. Her besom was found lying on the parapet by the perplexed police.

Crazed old woman thinks she is a witch and hurtles to her death, shrieked *El Periodic*. Alicia knows better. Her gran had been summoned by the Goddess.

Alicia is flying over that self-same parapet of the Casa de la Vall, the dove towers of the seat of government reaching towards her. There they beat, judged and hanged her ancestors during the bad times: times when they called the hooded inquisitors up from Spain to spread their venom throughout Andorra. She thinks she sees a shadow move at its base, but then the moon rises another notch into the sky and it vanishes. 'See you Àvia,' she calls in a high, thin voice that causes cattle to stir anxiously in nearby byres. There are still fields and farms not yet consumed by the city.

Tomorrow the farmer will blame yelping vixens for a failing milk yield.

Alicia turns with a jubilant whoosh of air, and heads away from the moon and north.

Descending over Anyós, her village, she sets the broomstick on course towards a drab huddle of tall buildings. A lot of trapped misery lingers there, but most powerful are the waves of gloom rising up from the top of one of the older blocks of flats.

In the cramped room, moonlight stripes the bed like prison bars. Nuria has her back to Josep, called after Josep of Arimathea, that great wizard, in the hopes that the Power would come to him. Alas, the laws of witchcraft are as arbitrary as those of human courts.

Poor Josep, she thinks looking down on him, starfished as he had slept since infancy. If he'd had the Power, things might have been different, and he would not have lain there, retired early from the Bank for some suspected, petty dishonesty. Nuria compelled to return again to teaching at the Lycée has not forgiven him.

Moving closer, Alicia sees that one hand is flung out against Nuria's bony back in a gesture which might have been construed as affection, had she not felt Josep's murderous dreams circle his wife, and smelt the corrosive bitterness of her loathing.

She bends over him and is astonished to find him so old, so withered. Gently she touches his lids, her lips move in the song she used to sing him to sleep with. The man's narrow lips relax, the eyelids smooth over the flickering eyeballs; for a moment the years peel back revealing the ghost of her bonny son.

Tomorrow, perhaps, he will, on an impulse he poorly understands, kiss his wife's lined cheek, and she will soften towards him. Alicia can do no more, except whisper goodbye.

Next, she stops above the church of Sant Cristòfol on its rocky outcrop a little apart from the village. It has endured since the eleventh century, its primitive stone bulk guarding the village, and the small town in the valley below. She flinches at the lights festooning the square tower and drowning out the gleam of moonlight on the crowning cross: lights designed to catch the attention of tourists, but more often a beacon to guide drunks home.

The wrought iron gates to the cemetery behind the church are locked but she enters without difficulty. She pauses before the high walls in which are filed the dead. Here, side by side, in the narrow spaces they lie; her parents, her sisters, her daughter and even her grandson who'd shown some promise in the Old Arts.

'Ah,' she sighs, tracing the script on a brass plate. 'Pere, Pere, I told you that drugs and motorbikes don't mix.' Slowly she moves down the row caressing each name like a mother bidding her many children goodnight. Last of all a kiss for Nuria, the injured one.

Then, leaning on her besom, she leaves the churchyard and hobbles down the grassy slope to where a leafless silver birch stands in perfect grace and a dark wild privet stinks of fox. She halts, panting, by a tangle of plants in which she props her besom. She is pleased that the rising moon still lights up the discreet cross placed there so long ago by her own hand.

The kind Mossèn had helped her with the cross, and when she looked at the priest, astonished, he had murmured that Christ had mercy for all.

'Well, Cris,' she whispers, 'it's been a very long time.' Cristòfol is the name inscribed on the cross. Any who happened upon it would think of someone named after the Saint of the village and travellers, but her fierce, savage husband had been given this name because *Cristòfol* had also been one of their own people; one who rejected the Dark One to serve the Lord.

'But the Dark One was too strong for you, beloved' whispers Alicia. She still calls him beloved, because she cannot forget that she had once delighted in his glorious beauty, returning his crazed love with an equal, untamed passion.

'Forgive me,' she says, kneeling down awkwardly so that her face is on a level with the cross. 'I had to do it, once you started to look at Nuri in that famished way. And you were fortunate. The Hemlock gave you a swift death. Poor Nuri died slowly of sorrow.'

In fact Nuria, young wife and mother, died of cancer; but Alicia is a firm believer in cause and effect.

She stays, kneeling, her head tilted as if to hear something. When at last she rises, her shoulders are slumped, and her face, etched by the ever-rising moon, is not that of a woman shriven. She sighs and picks from the tangled bushes a late, frost-seared rose, which she thrusts into her hair, and then, besom in hand, makes her stumbling way back up hill.

Ah how well she knows this church; her people have married here, baptised their young; been buried here although in the old days there had sometimes been murmurs of protest from the other villagers. She strokes the stone, rests her cheek against its roughness.

'Cristòfol, give me strength,' she whispers. The Mother Church has cut the giant from its litany of Saints, but she calls on him as a brother. 'Farewell,' she whispers to the village as she rises in the air and the wind embraces her skin with an icier touch; the besom seems harder to control than ever before. She is weary. She will take this last spin through the dazzling night, then home.

It is some distance to the house. On the way she crosses the lake called Engolasters, Star-Swallower, a silver plate below. She remembers their mid-summer revels, the power of the sun absorbed into their bodies as they danced to the sunrise, so young, so strong. Most of her people avoid the lake now and leave it to those who come and dance naked, make love, and claim rash kinship with the old ones.

The fools deserved the next day's snuffling colds and rheumatism.

Alicia flies along a road which she remembers as a track. It is a long time since she was here and she is amused by the tree-decked roundabouts and enchanted to see plaster wolves, bears and startled deer. Her laughter is young as she comes down close to the statues which quiver and twitch beneath her gentle breath. She soars up again, her laughter streaming behind her like a banner.

The next day a motorist will swear that he saw a Siberian wolf in pursuit of a brown bear. Another will declare that a deer must have escaped from Naturlandia.

The motorist will be arrested for the theft of the figures. He will be released for lack of evidence. The other man, a well-known figure, will be listened to with gravity but after counting the deer in the animal park and finding that they tally, it will be assumed that some creature strayed over the border, or else the important man had consumed a little too much good champagne.

Alicia is now above the gentler, wooded mountains of the south and moving towards a fertile plateau where an old house lies cradled amid potato and tobacco fields. The moon strikes wide windows broadside on and they glow back like messages of joy. The surrounding orchards are traceries, the slumbering flower-beds promise soothing potions once summer returns. Protecting rowan trees stand root-deep in wizened berries.

In the first bedroom, she sits on a chair by the wide bed and stares at Angels, the grandchild she'd reared after Nuria's death. The blond hair is streaked with silver now, the face unlined and tranquil. Angels holds her husband's hand in hers against the pillow. After a while, she stirs, and opens her eyes.

'I knew you would come. Why so long?'

'My powers are not so great now,' says Alicia. 'They are leaving me, to go to another.'

'You gave some to me,' whispers Angels.

'I was younger then, with energy to spare.'

'That is what it is?'

'Directed energy,' says Alicia. 'You have directed yours

well.' Her granddaughter is a holistic practitioner and a noted healer.

'So did you.'

'Not always,' says Alicia. 'I did no harm, save once, and maybe that was a dark good. But I let harm happen.'

Angels does not whisper her grandfather's name but briefly a shadow blocks out the moon and a figure seems to stand between them. 'Where are your powers going?'

'Come with me.'

Angels releases her husband's hand and slides from the bed. She follows her grandmother out of the room and down the corridor. Alicia stops at a half-open door, enters and kisses the sleeping youth tenderly. She moves on and enters a room where the curtains are wide-open and a girl lies in a puddle of moonlight. She stirs at the presence of her mother and her great-grandmother, but she does not wake.

'There,' says Alicia, 'can't you feel it?'

Hands stretch out to the sleeping girl. The three figures are like marble in the tremulous light.

Angels' voice is a little afraid. 'I never thought it would be Angela.'

'It was my last request of the Lady. Sometimes, She is kind.' Alicia takes Angels' hands in her own. 'Don't worry, dear heart, Angela will be great, and good.'

'And you, what ...?'

'I shall go now.'

'Shall I ride with you?'

'Not tonight.'

They are back in the bedroom where the man still sleeps. Alicia turns back the covers and Angels slides obediently in as if she were a child again. 'Sleep,' says Alicia, kissing her.

Angels sleeps.

Outside, the moon is far up in the heavens, shadows have darkened in the protecting garden, but still the windows flash their joyful messages, and the joy is reflected in Alicia's face.

She strides the besom and, with a last look, rises through air which seems to freeze her meagre flesh to her bones. She recalls long-ago nights when, curved against Cris's strong back, she hurtled across mountains and through the starry dark enfolded in his warmth.

Then was then, she thinks as the besom obeys the insistent pull of the moon, leaving the mountains, her mountains, far below, a silver sea. Her joy has become an agony as stars plunge past, then weave around her. The moon's dazzle blinds her. Within her frail old breast, her heart is a savage creature reaching out to whatever lies beyond the light.

Alicia stretches out her arms to the moon.

'How young she looks,' they will say the next morning. Mireia's small twinge of conscience that she was not there when Alicia lay dying will be assuaged by that calm face with its moon-blanched beauty. 'She had an easy death,' she will say to Angels and Angela when they arrive.

The two women will smile and nod as they stroke Alicia's cold hands, and Mireia will think that their tearless eyes are due to the fact that Alicia was so very old, and that really, it was time.

#9 FESTIVAL

31st October: Castanyades and Panellets & 1st November: All Saints Day

Originating some sixteen centuries ago, All Saints Day, or Tots Sants, is celebrated on the 1st November.

In days gone by, campanologists used to toll the church bells all through the night to remind the people of Catalonia to pray for the souls of the departed and for those uncounted millions still lingering on in purgatory. To make sure the bell-ringers didn't fall asleep on the job, friends and family would ply them with high-energy foods, hence the roasted chestnuts, sweet potatoes and *panellets* traditional at this time of year. You will also note a rare sight for Andorra: street vendors with permits to sell newspaper cones of hot roasted chestnuts and sweet potatoes off their little wrought-iron carts parked by the roadside.

In Andorra and Catalonia the main Castanyades or chestnut celebrations have now moved to the Eve of All Saints, also known as All Souls, the 31st October which is, of course, Halloween, which itself originated as a pagan festival celebrated by the nations of today's United Kingdom.

For *panellets* you need to go to a pastry shop or supermarket or alternatively make them yourself. The main ingredients are ground almonds and refined sugar mixed to a paste, or marzipan. Sometimes potato is added to help the ingredients go further. The mixture is then shaped into little cakes. There are many variations of *panellet* but the most popular is when the ball of marzipan is rolled in pine nuts, varnished in egg white and popped in the oven for long enough to lightly brown the nuts. Traditionally, *panellets* are accompanied by a sweet wine such as Muscatel.

THE DAY WE RAN SHORT OF VIRGINS

FICTION

by Ursula Simpson Ure

I lie awake at night and I hear a loud sigh. Then a groan. There is a prolonged creak. I do not put the light on, reach for a pistol or leap out of bed to confront the intruders. I know who they are. I lie awake for a while until all is quiet. I have been listening to the laments of the spinster virgins of Andorra.

When we built this house my father wanted only local wood to be used. There was no problem for the pine which came from Ordino and some of the master beams from Quillan in France, but he also wanted oak and walnut for panelling and furniture and stair treads. Our carpenter, Eroles, who was indeed a master cabinet-maker, told us he could find oak and walnut but it would take him several weekends on his friend's motorbike. He would have to go up into some of the more remote villages. Ramshackle pickup trucks and old vans with the doors at the back tied with rope duly appeared and our carpenter would triumphantly show my father the seasoned boards he had purchased. These loads vanished down the lane into his workshop and returned to us in the shape of polished panels and cabinets which he and his assistant, José, banged and hammered and coaxed into place.

One day he appeared looking worried. "We're running short of virgins," he said to me. "José and I spend nearly every Sunday calling on them. I just hope we have enough

236

for your father. I have been through nearly all the elderly ones."

"Did he say virgins?" my father enquired. "What have virgins got to do with me?" he asked Eroles.

"Well virgins or not, who knows? But all these on my list are elderly, unmarried ladies, and there are only one or two left that we can visit."

"I don't understand this," my father said. "What has *festejando las viejas* got to do with my house? And why does he want old ones? Nice looking fellows like him and his pal José should be after the young pretty ones."

When I translated this, Eroles shook his head. "No, no the young pretty ones are no good at all! The older the better, especially if they are from a good house." He produced a list and pored over it. "Well," he said, "Let's hope these three will be lucky for us." And he dashed off.

After the weekend he came to us, beaming. "I have been to Can so and so and Cal something and …" He reeled off various Andorran house names with gusto. "I think they are the last of the accommodating virgins. I've sometimes had to go back two or three times to convince them." He paused, eyes glinting. "Even when they are quite old and, you would think, resigned in their fate they don't want to admit it. But then I always tell them how beautiful your house is. One or two of them may come down to have a look. You don't mind do you?"

"I hope they're not coming to sue me or charge our friend here with rape! What has he been up to? He's not some sort of kinky *lothario* who only likes elderly ladies is he? What's this all about?"

237

Eroles' eyes were twinkling and he was hugely amused when I told him of my father's fears for his morals.

I could see he was curious. "No, no I don't go to *festejar* the old ladies. All I'm after is their wood! Whenever a girl child is born her father chooses and cuts down a fine oak or a walnut, or both, and stores the planks in his barn to make her wedding furniture. The ones who never marry often still have the wood stored away. It's the ones over sixty I want as the wood is really well seasoned and they haven't much hope of needing it to make bridal beds and chests and wardrobes. Some of them get very upset, however. They still have hopes I suppose while their walnut and oak awaits them in the barn. It's very difficult to persuade them to part with it but I take catalogues with me to show them. Modern furniture they can buy in La Seu or Leida or from Valencia, and the fair price I offer them, usually cheers them up."

"No one, I tell them, makes furniture out of these massive old boards any more. You go and pick out all this glossy, light, ready-made stuff, just as it suits you. It's much more showy. Of course I always say your father is a bit mad and he wants it all for doors and floorboards because he has a thing about oak and walnut – some people are a little crazy like that."

He told of one woman who had agreed to sell and then stood weeping while her walnut jolted away down the rough road from her house. Another questioned him minutely about this foreigner and his house for which her wood was needed and was quite upset when Eroles sketched her a picture. "Oh but that's just like any of our old houses and there's nothing marvellous about that." We were both amused and grateful that he should have taken such pains on our behalf.

The truth was that he loved oak and walnut as much as my father, who had been brought up in a family house in New Zealand built of seven different kinds of wood all of which he could name and describe. Eroles honed the old planks lovingly and brought them up to a wonderful patina. His deep waxing is still perfect and only needs an occasional rub.

The Andorran oak is a lovely warm colour and the walnut is marvellously patterned.

I lie awake and when I hear the sighs and groans, the soft lament of wood weeping, I give thanks and I am grateful for the virgins of Andorra.

10 FESTIVAL

THE CHRISTMAS SEASON

Decorations. Nowadays, street decorations begin to sprout even before the start of the ski season, around the beginning of December. More distinctive, however, are the nativity scenes or p*essebres*, depicting the countryside and the Bethlehem stable in which Jesus was born. There's an annual competition for the most intricate and life-like home-made scene; while the major churches have large layouts which attract children and adults alike. With moss for grass and tiny rocks for boulders, little running streams and waterfalls (and hidden electric pumps to circulate the water), camels bearing the Three Kings coming from afar, tiny stoneware jugs, the wooden manger with the minute figure of baby Jesus, each scene looks as real as possible. And crouched in there somewhere is the "caganer".

The Caganer or 'shitter', is a little squatting terracotta figurine with its pants down. Originally a farmer but nowadays he is as often a famous politician, a footballer, even the Pope or an Andorran 'conseller' - member of parliament wearing a black tricorn hat, as found on the packets of 'Conseller' coffee. The Caganer is usually tucked away, squatting, half hidden in a corner of the traditional crib scene so the children have to really search to spot him. He was originally said to bring fertility and good luck.

Caga Tió. So what's all this about 'Caga Tió' (*'Shit log'*)? As Christmas approaches you will see him all over the place. A small wooden log, usually with two legs in front, he lurks with his cheery grin and *barretina* hat, in the corner of shop windows or on sale at Christmas street markets. The Tió started bringing nuts to Catalan-speaking children some three hundred years before Father Christmas arrived to fill their stockings.

Originally the Caga Tió was just a large log that was brought into the home on the day of the Immaculate Conception, 8th December, and slowly fed into the fire till Christmas Eve.

Later, someone painted a smiling face on the flat end of the log, put a barretina on his head (the traditional red knitted Catalan hat) and laid a blanket over his lower back to keep him 'warm' at night.

The children had to take great care of Tió for he was a magic log. Every night until Christmas Eve they put out water and food for him: perhaps orange peel, potatoes or turron (nougat). Not only would the Tió log eventually bring warmth and light to the hearth but, the more they filled him up with food the more, hopefully, he would shit nuts and sweets for them on the night of Christmas Eve.

Finally the big moment arrives. Each small child is armed with a short stick. Maybe their father will take them off to the kitchen there to slightly warm their sticks in the oven; basically anything to get them out of sight of Tió where the mother quickly hides chocolates, nougat, Neules (very fine, rolled up, cigar-shaped Christmas biscuits) and other sweets and small presents under the blanket.

Once ready, the children are called back to stand around the Tió and sing to him whilst tapping him with their sticks. There are almost as many Tió songs as there are households. One goes like this:

"Caga Tió, neules i torrons,
Si no cagues ara …
cop de bastó!!!
Caga Tió!"

"Shit Log, neules and torrons
If you don't shit right now…
You'll get hit with a stick!!!
Shit Log!"

To begin with the children tap the log quite gently but at the final "Caga Tió" they hit the log really hard and then look under the blanket to see if he has pooped sweets or small presents for them.

http://www.youtube.com/watch?v=e4_oez7v9mM

24th December, Christmas Eve.

Father Christmas, a fairly new addition to the festive season, is welcomed into each parish in the early evening accompanied by assorted helpers: elves, gnomes etc. He usually arrives in the town's main square and mounts onto a stage covered by a marquee. There he sits down to receive the children's letters of good wishes and requests.

The Missa del Gall or Cockerel Mass sees Andorra's Catholic churches packed to standing room only. (Usually held at midnight, the Cockerel Mass recalls the fable that a cockerel was the first to announce the birth of Jesus. Traditionally the Song of the Cockerel opened the service.) A little before midnight the bells ring out and everyone heads for church. But not before leaving a good fire in the hearth and a stool beside it in case the Mother of God wants to come in to warm her hands. After the Mass most parishes offer mulled wine, hot chocolate and cake to warm the people on their way home.

THE APPRENTICE

FICTION

by J. P. Wood

A spray of dirty snow as he stamped on the rough wood of the threshold. The crooked chimney where it exited through the narrow window was warm to his hands and he followed it towards the blackened stove in the middle of the room. He sniffed the air.

Peret lumbered over. 'Only bar in the village still burning cow-shit.'

Jordi shrugged. In the sweet fuggy warmth beneath the metal tube, his child-self dozed sweetly until his Ma came to take him home, her rough hand warm on his.

'So what's up?'

'Tell you over a drink,' said his cousin.

'Better get on with it.' That brandy-laden breath boded trouble.

'Plenty of time.' Peret sauntered towards the bar where his father, with increasing volume, cursed the useless old bastard, Franco, taking Spain to perdition in a donkey cart.

'Deux vins rouges, cher Papa.' Peret leant his elbows on the bar, bringing himself down to his father's level.

Oh Lord, thought Jordi, sidling nearer the door. That atrocious French was just to provoke.

'You've had enough,' his father said in Catalan. Turning his shoulder on his son and heir to face his patient audience; 'Then we've got the fucking foreigners. Coming here, buying up good tobacco-growing land. Fucking greedy fools, selling. Soon there'll be no land, no tobacco – nothing.'

'Come on Pa. If you had anything you'd sell faster than a tart could drop her drawers.'

'Watch your foul tongue, boy.'

'Pot calling kettle black, Pa.' He jingled his hand in his pocket. 'Got the money.'

'And where from, I ask?' Another boiling look. 'No job, at least nothing you dare talk about, and still at home at twenty-four. Holy Mother, at your age ....'

Peret made violin playing motions, swiped a bottle of wine from the bar top.

'Put that down you ....' Pere reached out a long arm, but his son backed away. 'Besides, he's too young.' He yelled across to Jordi. 'Why aren't you studying?'

'Left school.' Repeat a year with all those clever clogs from the year below? Girls most of them. No thank you. 'Going to be an apprentice. Carpenter.' Was he? When his mother had suggested she could get him a job in old Toni's wood yard he'd screeched in protest.

'More fool you, and more fool you keeping company with this ne'er-do-well.'

Peret tossed a coin on the bar. 'Never say I don't pay my debts.' At the door, he snaked an arm around Jordi's shoulder. 'We shan't stay where we're not wanted. Crap place, anyway. Do something with it, Pa. Get a juke-box.'

'Juke-box!'

'Yeah, or a telly. Then maybe when Barça's knocking the shit out of Madrid, folks'll stay here instead of buggering off to Joan's.' He reached out for a bar stool, gave it a twist and the legs did a little pavanne on the uneven flagstones. 'At least you don't risk breaking your arse there.'

'You just go to Joan's.' Pere moved round the bar with surprising swiftness.

The kitchen door opened, the old cauldron suspended over the fire tossed out perfumes of stewing meat and onions. With practised skill Merce moved out to place her solid self between her two men.

'You two out,' she said, not ungently. 'And Pere, old Manel's dying of thirst.' As the young men slid out of the door. 'Peret, I expect you home in time to help clear up.'

'Not fucking likely,' said Peret as they leant against the low wall at the end of the village. He thumped the bottle on the wall and as the cork rose, yanked it out with teeth as white as the snowy fields. 'Better fish to fry.'

'What,' said Jordi, who'd received his cousin's summons through his mother when she returned from the big house.

'Cheek of the boy,' she'd said. 'Just as if I were a secretary.' But she'd smiled. She was fond of Peret, for all his naughty ways.

Peret took a long thoughtful swallow. 'Shit awful stuff. Here.'

Jordi took a cautious sip, grimaced, took another and felt the night chill ebb.

Peret grabbed back the bottle. 'You're not really going to work for that ponce?'

No need to ask who he meant. The business would soon belong to Toni the son, for money was no barrier to the cancer nibbling his father away, or at least so said Jordi's mother. She'd nursed Toni the younger when he was a baby, and had cooked and scrubbed there since her husband died, leaving her with a teenage daughter and a toddling boy.

'Good trade, carpentry.' He stared at his cousin, years of servitude stretching achingly ahead.

'You can't work for him. He was at school with me. He's a prize ...' Peret shook his head. 'Do you realise, that ponce's got a Jeep, a real Jeep and he hardly ever takes it out of the garage.'

'You've got the Moke.' He thought his cousin's Mini-Moke just the most desirable thing in the world.

'That's just it.'

'Just what?'

'The Moke's stuck just above Tor... Spanish side. That's why I need you.'

'Shit.' Spain, a dangerous, fearful place, full of sinister men who wore their hats sideways and shot to kill. Why his mother's cousin's uncle, hadn't he ... 'Can't you leave it till daylight?' Stupid question, judging by Peret's glare. 'Things you don't want the Guardia to find?'

'The pigs can trace the Moke to me. Could mean another spell inside.' For a moment he seemed to concentrate on extracting one last drop of wine from the bottle, tossed it over the wall which Jordi took to indicate there was nothing but a Sahara left inside. 'Hey man, work for me. I really, really need your help. I'll go thirty – seventy with you.'

'Fifty-fifty,' said Jordi, showing a trace of the businessman he would become.

Peret looked down at his cousin's shoes. The cracked leather formed craters in the dim light.

'Boots at home?'

'No boots.'

His mother said there was no money; true, but also in some way a punishment. Imma promised to buy him a pair with her first teaching pay-packet but some things were beyond the pale.

'I'll manage.'

The first part of the journey was pleasant, a half-moon peering over the mountain ridges and reflecting back off the fields. Jordi's torso was snug enough in his father's old sheepskin jacket. The track to the pass ascended gradually and, unlike Peret, he was light enough not to fall through the snow-crust. Next to him, Peret puffed and grunted, and spoke very little.

At the top, they paused for a moment, sweating, and Peret cupped his hand round a cigarette in the way of old lags. Jordi who'd tried smoking and disliked it stared around into the night. At school, sometimes they'd camped and watched the August rain of stars, but he'd been more intrigued by the giggling girls than the dazzling torrent of meteorites. Now he found himself intoxicated by the amphitheatre of mountains, ice-white in the ice-white light, the dizzy sweep of the lower slopes plunging into the darkness of the valley.

'Smuggling's a good job.'

'Loot, cars, girls, and booze,' agreed Peret.

And adventure, thought Jordi, and these mountains which are here for me.

'No more talking,' commanded Peret. He looked up to the slopes to their right, spoked and fringed by pines. 'This is real avalanche country.'

'Still too cold,' said Jordi, who also was a country boy, and besides in that lovely night, invulnerable.

Trudging behind Peret, in deep silence, except for the slither of snow and the occasional owl heckling the night, the enchantment continued the length of the long, flat track, the air sifting easily through his fit boy's lungs, his heart high and flying with the noisy owls.

Then they were through the rocky portals into deeper shadows and after a while, the track, left unkempt by the border police, became uneven, ambuscades of boulders lying under snow untouched by sun. Several times they both fell, and once Jordi sank up to his waist into a rock-bracketed drift and had to be hauled out by Peret who swore under his breath. He stumped on and Jordi realised from his hunched shoulders that the cheer of the brandy and wine had evaporated. His own joy stayed with him though his shoes had given up their role in life, letting the cold seep in.

Peret stopped at the top of the slope, his head cocked against the night sky. 'Up here, I think,' he whispered, not just for fear of avalanches, but for fear of passing patrols. Moonlit nights were a temptation to the nosy frontier police who frowned upon such fellows of fortune as they. 'Hurry your arse up.'

Jordi hurried his arse, and arrived panting to see the Mini-Moke half on its side in a streamlet. The small torrent had already congealed around two of its wheels. The others reached imploringly upwards. This will take some getting out, thought Jordi.

Peret waded into the stream, heaved out an army rucksack, slung it over to Jordi.

He wriggled the rucksack onto his back, helped Peret fasten another over his own broad shoulders, but not before his cousin extracted a bottle which glinted in the moonlight as he tilted it to his lips.

Probably how the Moke had ended up in the stream.

Jordi straightened up. 'Mother of God, what's in them?'

'Mostly fags and brandy. There's a guy down in La Seu takes them from me. He'll have to do without.'

The heavy rucksacks full of spite pushed them faster and faster down the treacherous terrain. Peret, slightly behind, grasped Jordi's jacket and pulled him behind a small rock and down into snow and dead bracken. His gloved hand pushed Jordi's grunt of surprise back down his throat, and remained in place, chafing his nostrils, until the sweeping lights of a jeep passed up the main track with a rumble.

'Thought so: the bastards couldn't resist.'

'Perhaps they are the others ...'

'Others?'

'Like us.'

'Don't want to meet those. You've a chance of surviving the Guardia.'

'Ah!' He was entering a place he didn't want to be.

'We'll have to go by the valley.' Peret looked at the steep and no longer moonlit drop below them and in answer to his cousin's unspoken question. 'The buggers will be back, and once we're on the main track, there's no way to go – except over the cliff or up the cliff.'

That of course, without wings, would be difficult, besides which there was no arguing because Peret was sliding and slithering over the edge. Following, Jordi found it impossible to keep to his feet on the frozen snow, and so he sat, the rucksack bumping behind him. Looking back, Peret did the same.

There they went, tobogganing down the steep valley flank, snow accumulating in their waistbands as they gathered speed. The track with its dangerous vigilantes was far above them, and they started to laugh like crazed creatures. Faster and faster they careered, and harder and harder they laughed, tears freezing on their cheeks.

Tomorrow, Jordi would have bruises on his arse, the shape and almost the size of continents. But now was now, and he was flying.

Through glittering waves of snow, he heard his cousin shouting, but the whoosh of air in his ears drowned out the words. Then his cousin was no longer there. He realised he'd been told to stop, couldn't stop. Before him lay darkness.

The darkness was cold, suffocating. It was all hard edges, it was wet. The river, in summer a stream, had taken a charge of snow and was in spate.

He surfaced and saw the black bulk of his cousin on the bank, arms upraised. 'Make for the road,' shouted Peret against the rackety waters.

Jordi was almost sure he heard the clank of bottles as his cousin turned and pounded upstream.

Bottles! He let go of the rucksack which his iced fingers hardly knew they still clutched. The bulk of a projecting rock on the other side promised safety and he struggled against the current towards it. He gave an involuntary grunt of horror as something soft and quite large thumped into him. A dart of moonlight revealed open but unseeing eyes. He caught at the sharp edges of glittering rock, held on, and the horrid corpse slid past, not the body of an executed smuggler, but a poor drowned dog. With a wriggle, he heaved himself up, too numb to feel the ripping of his trousers, the scraping of skin.

Horror again. On the rock were three tiny frozen corpses, each whisker, each clump of fur, each closed lid, silvered by moonlight.

One of the corpses wiggled, squeaked. Jordi was not the only one determined on life. He tucked the creature into the front of his sodden jacket. On auto-pilot, he clambered up the bank and into the moon-drenched field, beyond which he knew lay a village, very small, and by reputation somewhat given to incest and murder. He made for the road above it, his sodden clothes beginning to gleam. Perhaps anyone still awake in the village would take him for a ghost.

On the road leading back into Andorra, a solitary car passed, driven by a policeman who knew his mother. He left Jordi at the door of the woman with whom he had once been in love, and drove on, his back stiff with unasked questions.

Jordi's mother, sitting by the dying fire, asked no questions either, but stripped his soaking clothes from him, hanging them to dry by the chimney. Nor did she say a word when she saw the limp small dog stuck to her son's hairless chest. She dried them both with the same rough towel, fed them both hot milk, the puppy's ration from a baby's bottle. She smiled a little when her son refused the offer of some medicinal brandy.

'I shall call her Aigua,' said Jordi.

His mother nodded. This would not be a dog kept for guarding the house or sheep, rather a gift to her son who was a good boy and found life difficult.

She put him to bed with some old coats for extra warmth, and a hot brick at his feet. A sack on the floor for the pup but she would not have been the least surprised to know that as she closed the door, Jordi was already hauling the puppy up. Nor would she have been surprised that Jordi concluded smuggling was not the career for him. It would

253

have to be the big house and all that implied. The puppy licked his face and her heart ticked against his and it did not seem so terrible.

And you, dear reader, don't be too sorry for Jordi. He will enjoy working with wood, adore the scent and textures of felled trees and be a highly successful master carpenter. Young Toni, he will find to be a good fellow under his designer shades and clothes, and something of another lost soul. When old Toni dies, not too long from now, his son will come out of his stifling village closet, leave Andorra for France where they will be more tolerant of his handsome Corsican lover. Jordi will lament Toni when he becomes one of the earlier victims of AIDS but he will appreciate the legacy of the saw mill and workshop. Eventually, he will become a popular mayor of his parish.

Everywhere he goes, he is accompanied by a descendant of the long dead, much loved Aigua.

I once went walking with Steven
Who strode the hills like a demon
Despite the hard climbs
And the sliding declines
On balance it worked out quite even.

DEATH OF A CHRISTMAS CAROL

by Ursula Simpson Ure

The Virgin Mary had come down the hill on her mule, guided ably by St. Joseph. The manger awaiting them was resplendent with hay, the angels were scampering around on the roof and up in the trees, shepherds poked at their sheep, dogs were cavorting, the smugglers enjoying a quick nip from bottle or wine skin, the Devil had his fireworks primed and little Uncle Jaumet, the comedy figure, was hilarious. Electricians were busy fixing the spotlights. Snow had begun to fall.

We had come along the mud road from Escaldes and it was like stepping inside one of those picturesque snowstorm globes children love. *'El Pessebre Vivent d'Engordany'* was in full rehearsal and promised as usual to be a great success.

The first winters we spent in Engordany in the 1950s were greatly enlivened by local enthusiasm for the nativity play. The thin angular figure of Esteve Albert i Corp, local bard and creator of the pageant, dominated the scene. With his granny's scarf around his neck, his long nose pink with emotion and the cold, his eyes alternately watering and flashing, his mittened hands gesticulating, he was everywhere. The simple verses he had penned were written and re-written to enhance the individual personalities among his protagonists.

There was an old house along the road pullulating with energetic Andalus children. These provided the hard core of angels and for days beforehand white crêpe paper, staplers, aluminium foil, wire and tinsel and old sheets, were much in demand. Esteve Albert had conceived the play as a rustic celebration, the little stone houses and lights of old Engordany provided the back drop and one of the fields below the cobbled path was the site for the hastily-erected manger. Sheep, chickens, dogs, children, donkeys and mules were all welcomed and joined in with a will.

Uncle Jaumet of Cal Panxut was the comedy star and had to roll down the hillside fighting with the Devil, who leaped upon him from behind a bush with fireworks blazing, to try and disrupt the celebrations. This Demon King was stoned and put to flight by the villagers, with all the angels cheering!

Among the angels was one bright lad whose mother never seemed able to cope; he never had a halo, his gown was disastrous and - Oh Shame! - he had NO WINGS! He was a tuneful singer and full of charm and the cry would go up when he was late for rehearsal -"*Dónde está Antonio? Antonio que no tiene alas!*" - Antonio who has no wings. All the other angels would gather him into their midst, he would be hidden and no one would notice his lack of celestial plumage, but inevitably he was known as the 'one without wings'. He was given wings which, however, never survived the attentions of his younger brothers and sister and brawling puppies. All sorts of efforts were made; he remained wingless but enthusiastic throughout the festivities.

In our *Pessebre Vivent* the smugglers were *much* to the fore, they were very popular and provided a lot of *business* with brandy kegs and packs of tobacco. One old boy would pull out from around his hairy chest, yards of Alençon lace, used for trimming ladies' underwear - and then make the spectators roar with delight as he guiltily stuffed it all back again. The villagers brought wood for the fire to warm the Holy family, milk for the baby and eggs and bread for the Virgin, a shepherdess gave wool from her sheep. They all brought gifts and praised the Child. It was acted with great simplicity and good humour, audience participation was paramount.

Then the road was made up and widened for traffic, blocks of flats shot up where only fields had been. The view down to the river was blotted out. The cosy village atmosphere was gone and with it our winter celebration.

Splendid Kings with pages and attendants now came along the tarmacadamed road and scattered bonbons. We had fairy lights and Christmas trees, reindeer and Ho, Ho, Ho!... No longer the gleam of torches on the hillside, the mule bearing the comely Virgin picking its way carefully down the track.

I listen still and I can hear once more the bell-clear notes of Antonio-without-wings up on the roof of that ramshackle stable, singing his heart out amidst the un-celestial choir, while the snow swirls softly, gentle flakes falling on bare open ground.

When choosing to ski 'en Andorre'
There's one thing je vous implore:
When zooming down-slope
On a prayer and a hope
Avoid slower folks going before

FAMILY FOUND

FACTION

by Iain Woolward

My father was a bastard, literally and figuratively. The stigma gnawed at him. Turned him mean. And by the time I got to know my mother she was already going literally out of her mind. With her there was no "figurative". Didn't have the wits for it. The two of them battled each other for about half a century, all told. Swatting and drinking. Drinking and swatting. Hitting targets that half the time they didn't even know were there. The pair of them still suck me down in dreams. I hug them, but it does no good.

I lit out of the household pretty young and left for America not long after; barely shaving. Scotland was all I'd known as a boy. The night before I left, I stood leaning against the breeze on a bluff overlooking the Firth of Forth, Edinburgh blinking in the distance to the south. Was it the wind in my eyes, or was I actually crying? Best not to think about it.

I was greatly aided in my escape by a man called Freddie Laker. Freddie ran a couple of 747's heading out west from Heathrow clear to San Francisco. Nowadays you'd call it a 'discount airline'. Back then you just called it 'cheap'. Hell, Freddie even suggested we all bring our own sandwiches lest we got hungry crawling through the sky over Greenland and the neighbouring tundra. So I did. Munched away, peering down at the emerald 'bergs' and wrinkled glaciers, earphones looping on Johnny Cash and Willie Nelson. By the time we reached San Francisco they were gone - the sandwiches that is. Swooping over the Golden Gate, pinnacles jutting through a low fog, something changed: I'd become American.

Back then, California was a place where damned near anyone with half a brain and an urge to do so could get ahead. So I did. Even got married a few times. Americans mostly. Probably a mistake: never could read 'em right. They'd get to philandering soon enough, pop the big 'Goodbye' and scuttle off with whatever they could grab. I guess I wasn't well-versed in the family way, not having lived it. So I worked away at other stuff; nose, grindstone and so on.

I was damned near fifty when I thought I'd give romance another shot. Hooked up with a Polish girl. She'd been in California a while, by way of the UK. Alicjia Bernadetta Josefina Celestina Jarawslava. Something to do with Saints days. I fell hard; the way her blue eyes turned black with her mood. You knew where you stood. Her skin was milk white; smooth, so smooth. She was old school; been raised by her Polish grandmother – a woman who'd single-handedly kept a roof over the heads of eight kids during World War II. When the Soviets rolled into southeast Poland the first order of business was to drag her husband and 25,700 other Polish servicemen off to the Mother Country, shoot 'em in the head and toss them into a big hole in the Katyn Forest. The women and children got shunted off in cattle cars to Siberia.

Post war, what was left of the family pulled itself up by its bootstraps as refugees in England. Alicjia was born in a camp to a mother who, by all accounts, was a waste of space – some put it down to being fed slop as a kid in the

Gulag. So daughter and grandmother ignored the middle generation and got real close. That's probably why Alicjia had a wisdom about her. A man could trust her. She'd married young, but hubby had died a few years back, leaving not much else but surprises: a big bunch of bills and mortgage payment demands that were all gussied up with red ink and double under-linings. Alicjia knew life could trick you into thinking it's easy when actually it isn't. She could handle herself.

Now, it was about this time that some big oil men down in Texas dragged little George 'W' Bush out from his playroom by the ear and popped him blinking and wriggling into the Oval Office. Pretty soon 'W' was making my skin crawl. When he weasel'd his way back into the White House for a second term things went from embarrassing to downright irritating; time for Alicjia and me to get the hell out of there and head back to Europe.

We skipped the UK - too many memories and a lot less 'united' than we recalled. Stateless souls, we wandered the sunnier climes of Europe thinking somewhere would call out to us. It didn't. By the time we'd covered most of the coastal territory between Dubrovnik and Barcelona, 'stateless' was becoming 'homeless' and homeless was becoming old. We needed a base.

A digression: over the years, I've concluded that, by and large, democratically elected governments lacked the collective DNA to responsibly manage our money. This had engendered in me an increasing disgruntlement at working Monday morning through Wednesday lunchtime just to pay Federal, State, and County taxes: income, sales, property, capital gains.....not much moves in The Land of the Free that's free of tax. And so I'd become increasingly curious about countries in which folks pay a hell of lot less taxes and get a hell of a lot more for them. I'd read that Andorra is such a country, and had been since Charlemagne gave it the thumbs up for statehood around 899 C.E. It was his way of saying 'thanks' for helping keep the Muslims from marching north, unopposed, through the mountain passes of the eastern Pyrenees. The Andorrans had proved good for the task – even though the Moors did make it half way into France by other routes before getting pushed back.

And so it was that Alicjia and I found ourselves high in those same mountain passes one crystal clear spring day, typical of these parts. We started poking around a country that has pretty much balanced its books for over a thousand years without taxing its populace more than 10% of their incomes.

But I'll be straight with you: at first, the big advantage of having a base in Andorra was that we could store a bunch of stuff in it, cook ourselves a solid meal and do some quick laundry before heading back out to look for somewhere else to live. Looking back, I put this down to the "Doctor Who" syndrome. As you may know, the good Doctor travelled through time in a vehicle – the Tardis - that looked a lot smaller from the outside than the inside. Andorra's a midget of a country. It's easy to think you've got a quick handle on it, when you ain't. It takes some getting to know. Drive in from Spain and the first stuff you see is...well... "depressing as hell" was how Alicjia put it, adding, "There's just no fucking way I'll live here." Strong stuff. Ordinarily she never swore.

The main town is all hunkered down like a scolded dog, cowering under steep mountains that have got it pretty much surrounded. The locals speak Catalan, a weird Spanish-cum-French concoction, lacking enough of either to get an untrained tongue around in a hurry. That alone could be a deal-breaker because, in our view, immigration and integration should be one and the same. Being Americanized, we were disinclined to seek out the English 'ex-pat' colonial community. (By the way, there are barely any Americans in Andorra; the banks won't touch 'em since the U.S. is hostile to any nation capable of running its affairs with less tax revenue than the U.S. thinks appropriate.)

Alicjia's orneriness notwithstanding, we set ourselves up in a hole-in-the-wall apartment (not unusual in these parts since a lot of the populated landmass is damn near vertical) and started a more extended tour of the country. Turned out the north end – the opposite end from our entry point from the Spanish border – is drop dead gorgeous. Tall mountains; rushing rivers; cute alpine villages and, compared to what we were used to, hardly any traffic. Indeed the place seemed deserted. (In spring, after ski season, everybody goofs off for a while). Strolling around, I could sense Alicjia's mind opening a crack. Getting back on the road to go look for a place somewhere else seemed less urgent. We upgraded to an apartment we could live with – available detached houses being like hens' teeth around here.

Pretty soon after that we quit thinking we could get to be bosom pals with the Andorrans - at least not until we learned Catalan. That would be a while; we were getting by

OK on wobbly French. So we got into tow with a bunch of English folks… or at least folks who'd lived in England yonks ago and bailed, never to return. With a few irritating exceptions, these were not British colonial types oozing the arrogance for which they're renowned around the globe - especially the bits upon which the sun never used to set. Hell, these folks were pretty much like us. They'd lived all over the world, worked their asses off, pulled down some money and paid their taxes. Now they wanted to hang on to what they'd earned and kick back a little. At the mention of 'big government' or 'nanny states', even I'd be looking for cover. These folks had long since taken responsibility for their own welfare in exchange for freedom on a scale that Andorra still provides.

Now, if you're wondering why this story is titled 'Family', it's this: Alicjia and I have met and grown close to - I mean really care about - more people in a couple of years in Andorra than in decades spent in what many folks might think were much fancier parts of the planet. These people have become the 'family' neither of us ever had. In a crunch they'd be there for us, without question. And vice versa. Yes, Andorra offers beautiful scenery and an orderly society rightly proud of the sovereignty and personal freedoms that they've defended for over a thousand years. But what makes this 'home' for us is a sense of 'family' that we'd never really had and never expected to find, but did. Family found.

Three young maidens from Erts
Were just the most terrible flirts.
When over they bent
The fellows were sent
Quite mad by their very short skirts

BECOMING ANDORRAN

by Clare Allcard/Thompson Foster

It all started with a baguette; well, that and a Communist coup.

In 1977, communist mercenaries seized power in the Seychelles, our Indian Ocean home. Soon they had allocated to themselves the right to commandeer any form of public transport they fancied. Fearing they might easily fancy *Johanne Regina,* our beautiful ex-Baltic trader, my husband Edward and I upped anchor and set sail for Singapore.

We arrived as tourists but wanted to linger longer and so I had to go every fortnight to Immigration to beg them on bended knees to renew our visas for "just two more weeks". Each time they required more convincing. A bureaucratic pain, but Singapore's boatyards and carpenters were impressive and our fifty-year-old wooden sailboat desperately needed attention.

Then I bought that serendipitous baguette. As usual, the baker had wrapped a scrap of newspaper around its middle for me to hold it by. And, as usual, on arriving home I smoothed out the scrap and began to read.

It was an advertisement from an estate agent called CISA based on the other side of the world in a country called Andorra. It invited readers to buy property there. I had never heard of Andorra but Edward had. He had once spent 24 hours there.

"It's a swindle!" he cried. "You go and ask them how much it rains! Never stopped raining when I was there!"

The next day I went to the hotel where CISA was promoting their properties.

My question surprised them. "Rain? I don't really know," replied the beautiful Malaysian woman at the desk. "Maybe 40 days in the year?" She then handed me leaflets showing various properties and gave me, in passing, the astonishing news that I would not need a visa to visit Andorra.

I carried the pamphlets – and the news - back to Edward. We had been considering returning to Europe for some time. Having abandoned our 17 acre coconut plantation in the Seychelles, we needed a new land base. And in Andorra we wouldn't require a visa! Could this be it? One house in particular caught our eye. Small, it stood all alone in an alpine meadow. Behind it fir trees rose towards a white, mountain ridge. It looked idyllic. Even the price was acceptable.

"Why don't you go and look at it? Mind you, we don't want to be able to hear any traffic or a neighbour's radio or a dog bark or see another house."

A couple of weeks later I arrived in Andorra with Edward's list of requirements in my hand.

It turned out that the photograph was old. The idyllic alpine meadow had sprouted six more houses. But my guide, the multilingual Dutchwoman, Arina de Reuter, did not despair. At least not quite. The main problem was dogs. At that time every other house seemed to boast a vociferous Alsatian. Each time we stopped the car, the dogs barked.

"Sorry! No good!" I would say and Arina would restart the engine and we'd set out yet again.

Finally she drove up a dirt track and halted beside a tiny orchard. No dogs! Also no house. The plot was minute but it was surrounded by communal land which could not be built on. We got out. Still not a dog to be heard, nor for that matter, a neighbour's radio for there were no neighbours and, provided one looked in the right direction, no houses to be seen either. An hour's survey revealed just one car passing along the little road below. We'd found it!

I flew back to Edward with the information and, satisfied with my report, we chose CISA to build Xalet Hort Dret (Orchard on the right). Amazing how a baguette can change your life.

In 1986 we sailed back to Europe and Edward saw the house for the first time. He fell instantly in love with the view. Just as well: we counted 12 heavy lorries every hour thundering along that little road below, going to and from a (thankfully) soon-completed construction project. We also discovered that, when the wind came from the wrong direction, the sound of barking dogs wafted across the valley on the night breeze. But not to worry. By then Andorra had us hooked.

When we applied for passive residence, the woman at Immigration could not have been more charming. Her chief concern was that, after spending so many years gazing at the ocean's wide horizons, we would feel claustrophobic within Andorra's mountain folds.

"Not a bit of it," said Edward. "It's all part of nature. The mountains are just waves standing still."

The immigration officer smiled with relief. "In that case, go to the Govern and ask for Rosa. She'll help you with the paperwork." An immigration officer who would help? What sort of paradise was this?

Back in 1986 to become a Passive Resident in Andorra one had only to prove that one was healthy, had medical insurance, no police record and an income three times the minimum wage. (Today things are very different. For a start €400,000 is required either in the form of a deposit or the purchase of property. Alternatively you could try to set up your own business.)

After living in 19 different countries I began, for the first time in my life, to put down roots. And after 20 years of anchoring up lonely jungle creeks and in deserted tropical bays I joined everything: the International Club, local charities, hospital volunteers, the English-speaking Church... In 1989 I was part of the group that founded the International Singers (now El Cor Internacional d'Andorra). In 1993 I co-founded Andorra Writers' Circle and together we wrote the guide book: *Andorra: Festivals, Traditions and Folklore.* And yet I was still officially labelled a *Passive* Resident!

Six months after we arrived, Edward and I started Catalan classes, that being the official language of Andorra. But, as many foreigners discovered in those days, practicing Catalan in Andorra was tough. You'd say "Bon dia!" and even if the person was Andorran, they'd reply 'Buenos dias!' in Spanish. I thought perhaps it was some sort of ritual greeting like the beautiful Swahili one that begins "Jambo!" and ends, seven phrases later, with "asanti sana!"

As I was also trying to speak Spanish when on the boat down in Spain, I ended up totally confused and for the next 15 years spoke Spatalan.

Then the residence period for becoming an Andorran citizen changed from 25 to 20 years. Just two years away! For the first time I considered it seriously. I had left Britain in 1968. Andorra was my home, where my heart was. The country where people said "Bon dia!" as they entered a lift full of strangers and where the strangers chorused "Bon dia!" in reply. I had no intention of leaving, so becoming a citizen suddenly seemed obvious. I made a resolution to drop the *Spatalan* and only use Catalan from then on.

When my 20 years was up I applied for Andorran citizenship, despite the fact that it meant I would have to renounce my British – and thus EU – passport. (Andorra does not allow dual nationality nor does it belong to the EU.) I was informed that I would be cross-examined on Andorra's history, geography, politics, constitution et al - and in Catalan naturally. I started swotting up possible answers.

Meanwhile I had to order an apostilled birth certificate from the UK. As I handed the certificate to the Andorran policewoman she said, "You do know you will have to change your name?" For some reason my brain failed to hoist that in.

Just two weeks before the dreaded exam, I received a list of six Catalan books to read. Total panic! Even in English I'm hard pressed to get through more than one book a week.

On the appointed day, I went down to the Govern and joined some half-dozen other, highly nervous men and women perched on the edge of their seats. One by one they were ushered in – and out. Eventually my turn came. There, in a small room, sat six examiners. My heart pounded, my palms sweated. I hadn't taken an exam for at least 30 years. My greatest dread was that one of them would speak what I call '*wooje wooje*' Catalan (when the speaker never moves their lips at all and everything is a great furry blur).

An elegant woman in her forties began. She spoke beautifully - but so fast it felt like being machine gunned. How I blessed my friend, Maria Teresa Planàs, who for years had spoken to me at just that speed.

"Rosemary, what do you do in Andorra?" Oh no! I should explain. I was baptised Rosemary Clare Thompson. I was always called Clare, never ever Rosemary. For the past thirty-nine years, since marrying Edward, I had been Clare Allcard but, as the policewoman had warned, they had changed my name. I had become Rosemary (first given name) Thompson (father's surname) Foster (mother's surname). All those years of earning Brownie points as "Clare Allcard - Eager Volunteer" had gone for nothing. I wouldn't stand a chance!

"What do I do here? I suppose you could say I'm an obsessive volunteer. I volunteer for everything: a guide at international conferences and sports events, volunteer at the hospital. Most recently I organised Catalan classes for 35 retired English-speakers."

To one side of me, a man whispered "It's her!" Thank the Lord! Brownie points reinstated…

"How long have you been speaking Catalan?" Uh, uh! My Catalan is still far from perfect.

"Well you see, I started by speaking Spanish then tried to learn Catalan. For the next 15 years I spoke *Spatalan*." I heard an amused murmur. Clearly *Spatalan* worked in Catalan as well as English. "And then," I went on, "At the Millennium, I resolved to speak only Catalan."

More contented murmurs. Other questions: on the constitution, geography, history followed but from the look on their faces I had scraped through. Indeed I should say here that all six examiners could not have been kinder or more encouraging. I really felt that they *wanted* me to succeed.

Afterwards friends asked whether I thought I had passed. I replied, "If it is based on knowledge of Andorra, yes. If on my Catalan, no." It must have been based on my knowledge of Andorra.

The final sprinkle of star dust on the transformation came at a little ceremony when the then Head of Government, Albert Pintat, handed out passports to some thirty new Andorrans. I was the only Anglo-Saxon present.

"Rosemary Thompson Foster!" No one moved. I looked around. And then suddenly I realised – that's me! I went forward, smiled nervously and received my passport. I had become an Andorran.

> *You can live here ever so long*
> *And feel you don't really belong.*
> *But just learn the lingo*
> *And suddenly, bingo!*
> *It's amazing how you'll get along!*

PEARLS WITHIN REACH

by Iain Woolward

As a tourist I suck. If I haven't got a practical reason for going to a place... work, weddings, children's inexhaustible curiosity and so on... I'd rather not bother. If some such imperative has plopped me into, say, Florence or the Floridian Everglades, I'll poke around. But I won't go out of my way just so that I can say I've gondola'd down the Grand Canal or climbed the Statue of Liberty. So I actually *like* living in a country that has no national art gallery, looming cathedral or gaudy theme park: Andorra. There's tons of stuff to do here that doesn't involve shuffling and gawking one's way through some ancient building, just because it's ancient. In fact you'll be hard pushed to find a big crowd anywhere in Andorra. When the pavements of the main shopping boulevard started to get a little too congested for comfort, the local worthies diverted vehicular traffic so that pedestrians could safely spill out into the roadway. You can swing a cat on the main shopping avenue of Andorra on a Saturday afternoon and inconvenience nobody except the cat.

Imagine, then, my initial surprise when I was asked to write a short essay on the places of interest within an hour or two's drive from Andorra. But, of course, the logic was Einsteinian: if *I* found such a place worth a look almost anyone would. On top of my ineptitude as a tourist can be added thirty years in the advertising business. This has equipped me with an acute nose for hype of the kind I churned out for a living. Consequently, within nanoseconds of glancing at a rack of pamphlets in a hotel reception area I can spot the 'attractions' that will, in my opinion, leave the visitor gasping in disappointment - unless he or she is, for example, making a study of the world's smallest solar-powered boilers or largest arrays of smoked hog haunches.

What the following lacks in comprehensive coverage it will attempt to make up for with brutal honesty and admirable brevity. (I'm not about to waste my time or yours regurgitating stuff already accessible in profusion via Google).

Let's kick off in the Grotte de Niaux. I'd driven up from Toulouse to Andorra a hundred times before a visiting guest suggested we take a quick detour about half way between the two. Frankly I was gob-smacked: unlike other, better known stone-age caves where hoards of visitors – and their steamy breath - have so damaged the wall paintings that only copies remain accessible for public viewing, Niaux offers the real thing, up close and personal. Gaze across ten or twenty feet and back ten millennia. These guys were *good*: they didn't just scrawl some bison-like graffiti on a wall and step back, hands on hips, thinking they were hot shit. The drawings of bison on the walls of the vast Niaux cave not only go beyond mere representations: they have *personalities* – as had, no doubt, the people who created them. I can imagine groups of grunting, torch-bearing fans from all over the area clumping their way two kilometres (!) back into the cave to gaze in silence at these works of art before turning to give their slanty-browed Leonardo a slap on his – or maybe her - big hairy back. In more recent times fans could only express their appreciation by scrawling stuff on nearby walls; check out the graffiti from 1602.

Given the sheer size of the cave at Niaux (and others in the area), you may not be surprised by my next recommendation: Europe's longest, navigable underground river – the Labouiche at Vernajoul, near Foix (which history buffs might want to explore en route). About 1.5 kilometers of the Labouiche glide majestically 60 meters underground, as you'll see if you take a boat trip through the eerie rock formations.

And talking of rivers: where the rivers Tet and Cadi meet is the tiny, heavily fortressed town of Villefranche de Conflent, about 50 kms up into the Pyrenees west of Perpignan on the Mediterranean. (It's OK: you're not meant to have ever heard of these names – except maybe Perpignan. Oh, and the Mediterranean). It's from Villefranche (a UNESCO's World Heritage site) that The Little Yellow Train departs. Yes, that's honestly what it's called ('Le Petit Train Jaune'). But, before you write it off as an amusement ride dreamt up by Disney Paris for tiny totties, know this: riding this sucker 63 kms/39 miles up 1,592 metres/5,226 ft into the Pyrenees will be a lifetime memory. It's one of the world's most remarkable train journeys, which is why booking is a really good idea - as is not messing about on the electrified third rail of the 1 metre gauge railway.

Turning to the Spanish side: I'm going to skip Barcelona, stuffed as it is with points of interest for even the most reluctant tourist. It's covered extensively elsewhere and is about 30 minutes outside my brief of 'two hours drive from Andorra'.... but then so is my first Spanish recommendation: the Dali Museum in Figueres – near the Mediterranean coast, just short of the French border.

I've been dragged to many a museum by erudite friends, or been compelled by boredom to stick my face into them, having arrived early somewhere for some conference or other. (I'm more willing to fill in time this way in Britain because: a) they're free, and b) current exhibitions often crop up in local small talk; you can come off as an ignorant slob if you don't know what's going on at the Tate or Saatchi galleries). To overcome this problem in my busier and more athletic youth I'd combine jogging with art appreciation. Once I completed a circuit of *every* gallery of *every* museum on the Mall of Washington DC in less than an hour, stopping only to pant at items that took my particular fancy. It's surprising how much one can take in at the trot - or flat out run - through even the most esoteric exhibit areas. It's rather like how we can understand speech at eight times the speed at which we can emit it. There's actually no need to dawdle through museum galleries: your brain 'got it' pretty much the second you walked in. Once I was speed-walking through the Met. in New York and burst into tears within seconds of entering a gallery stuffed with (evidently) overwhelmingly gorgeous and equally famous impressionist art. My conscious self was shocked and embarrassed. I hurried on.

There's a tendency to creep around these places because we're as much on show as the exhibits: we need to *look* as if we are super-interested in poorly executed renditions of subject matter that has long since lost whatever fascination it engendered – if any – half a millennium ago. For example 99% of us find flat-faced Byzantine art terribly, terribly boring. Hell, the stone-age drawings at Niaux (above) are way better rendered. But this doesn't stop museums from begging for public money in order to clutter their walls with the stuff.

Dali understood all this. And he could really draw. Go to his museum. No doubt you're already familiar with a bunch of his work. What you may not know is that, unlike those who thought art should be housed in buildings that looked like Victorian asylums for the mentally ill, Dali dictated that, "My museum will leave those who come to see it with the sensation of having had a theatrical dream." And you will.

As further proof of Dali's prowess, go to the Picasso museum in Barcelona (again, outside the remit of this article). There you'll find every doodle the home-boy contrived as a youth. All rubbish compared to what his not-so-distant neighbour Dali was producing barely out of the cradle. The comparison is a tad unfair since Picasso was an iconoclast looking for a medium. He hung out with authors, but settled for odd-looking art as a way to shake things up a bit. Nevertheless, the museum is chock-a-block with gawkers assuming they should appear impressed.

It's tough to write about 'Spain' and 'Art' in the same piece and not tag on a bit about the Prado Museum in Madrid – one of the world's best for stuff you're sure to recognize. So let me at least touch on getting to Madrid from Andorra: most people drive to Lleida and jump on the high-speed train, the AVE. It'll take two hours and a shocking number of euros to get you to Madrid. Alternatively, driving the whole way is straightforward because it's a straight line from Andorra through Lleida and Zaragoza (a slurring of its original name: 'Caesar Augustus-ville', unlikely as that may now seem) to Madrid. It's an excellent road, but after Lleida it'll take you about twice as long as the train, if you obey the speed limit (which very few Spaniards seem to do on the Autopiste). Alternatively, you could 'do' Barcelona (2 – 3 hrs driving by bus or car from Andorra) and then go on to Madrid (2-3 hrs by AVE). In one day you'd be able to make a direct, hands-on comparison between Catalonian versus Castilian culture. Please: don't make the mistake of thinking Spain is one big happy family. They've only been experimenting with democracy since 1976 and are still working out the kinks. It's tricky: not too long ago one faction locked up half a million of the other faction in concentration camps and put a bunch of them to work mining fun stuff like mercury. Even though memories of Sr. Franco's rather humourless approach to national unity are fading, the two major cities still have very different styles, Barcelona being the LA to Madrid's much more reserved, say, Philadelphia. They still, literally, don't speak the same language.

If you do drive from Andorra to Madrid and get bored en route, take some time out to throw yourself off a cliff, or simply while away a pleasant afternoon watching others do so from the ridges above the village of Ager, not far from Lleida. It's a hang gliding and para-sailing Mecca, especially in the spring. There are four main launch points – all fanned by reliable thermal breezes from early spring and on through the summer. In fact the winds are so constant that 100km flights, back and forth along the ridges, all day long, are not unusual. All the sites are reasonably accessible by unloved rental car, via well maintained forest roads - one site is even serviced by Land Rover taxis from a nearby campsite. There's lots of opportunity to learn how to get the hang of hang gliding.....safely. Ager village itself is very cute, and really buzzes when a World or European hang gliding championship rolls into town.

A final note: I know people who settled in Andorra decades ago, having travelled extensively throughout all but, perhaps, one of the Earth's continents. They still haven't been to half the places I just mentioned. Perfectly happy messing about in good old Andorra, punctuated every now and then with trips to bustling Barcelona, or down the French side to Toulouse, plus the occasional foray to a Med resort, just to make sure the sea still sparkles.

The light fades, shadows
and lines merge, blurring edges,
veiling the way back.

Valerie Rymarenko

ACKNOWLEDGEMENTS

Our warm thanks go to:

Rosa Maria Beal, Josep Maria Camp, Pere Canturri, Fiona Dean, Simó Duró, Krystyna Filistowicz, Marc Forné, Hugh Garner, Antoní Garrallà, Maria Rosa Garrallà, Robert Garrallà, Andrés Luengo, Ann Matschke, Carolina Plandolit, Jordi Robert-Ribes, Annie Tee and Susanna Vela Palomares for sharing so much with us.

Also to Patricia Grey and members of the Andorra Writers' Group for their generous support.

THE COVER

Special thanks to Jimmy Turner and Jaume Riba Sabaté for the cover photos and Mark Lodge for the cover design and book formatting.

Printed in Great Britain
by Amazon